The Journey with Tom
MEMORIES OF AN ARIZONA PIONEER WOMAN

By
Alice Curnow
(1861 – 1940)

Edited by
Mona Lange McCroskey

Mona Lange McCroskey

HollyBear Press
P.O. Box 4257
Prescott, Arizona

© 2003
HollyBear Press

All rights reserved.
Printed in the United States of America

HollyBear Press
P.O. Box 4257
Prescott, Arizona 86302-4257
(928) 776-4689

ISBN:0-9651067-1-3

Library of Congress Catalog No. 2003107764

First Edition

Cover design and illustration by Western Icons.com
Book design by Becky Fulker.
Printed by Classic Prescott Printing, Prescott, Arizona.
Set in Zaph Calligraphic 801.

Silver King Stage, 1880s. *Arizona Historical Society/Tucson, #22223, Wood Collection.*

ARIZONA PIONEERS
By Alice J. Curnow

Down from the North and in from the East
    And up from the South came we.
Out of the West, from the Golden State
    On the shore of the placid sea.
We found our places and we did our best
    As we lingered a long, long while.
Helped to settle this state of the great Southwest
    The land of an endless smile.

We followed the trail that the prospector blazed
    In his search for the Realm of Gold,
Over a weary and tortuous way
    In a land that was grim and old.
And we marked where the fires of God had been
    When the molten world was young.
And we turned an ear to the fearful din
    Of the death the Apache sung.

Some went with their herds and learned the thrills
    That come from the dawn and the sunset's glow;
That come from the music of echoing hills,
    From the songs of pines when the soft winds blow.
In the Saddle from dawn till dusk
    They watched and tended and never shirked.
Whistling gaily they rode the range
    And did their part in the settlers' work.

Some chose the valleys where homes now stand
    Midst groves of orange and date.
A monument to the work of their hand
    When they labored early and late.
Now they sit in the shade of trellised vine
    And enjoy the fruits of their toil
While they spin their yarns of hardships endured
    In their fight to produce from the soil.

For real content you must make men happy
        With occasional fun; they will work more snappy.
So 'twas:
        Balance all and right and left
        Swing your partners and alamen left
        Wing the corners and round you go
        Balance your partners and do-si-do.

Something like this was the call they gave
        And never a thought of musicians to save;
As without a frown they sawed away
        From nine o'clock to the break of day.
Theirs was the part of giving pleasure
        And they did their duty in the fullest measure.

Last, not least, now comes the one
        Whose tasks were n'er finished at set of sun.
Whether on mountain, hill, or plain,
        By mill or mine her work was the same:
To make it a home that her mate provided.
        With heart and hand she faithfully guided
The comforting at the end of the day
        When weary he rested in the firelight's play.

There they welcomed the babies, one by one;
        Now a daughter and now a son.
And she grew in strength through their helplessness
        As she answered each cry of their keen distress.
There were days of sunshine and nights of fear
        With the Grim Reaper hovering near.
There were questions to answer and stories to tell
        While the castles she built oft' times fell.

Now she looks through a mist of happy tears
        Down the vista of those busy years,
As she views with joy her work well done.
        In her gracious daughters and noble sons.

Illustrations

Foreword

Alice Curnow likely thought of herself as an "ordinary" woman. Like most of her Victorian peers, she devoted her life to establishing a comfortable, peaceful home for her husband and children. The fact that the house was sometimes nothing more than a canvas-sided structure with a dirt floor was not remarkable in the era of western migration and boom-and-bust gold rushes. Flash floods, the threat of Indian attacks, severe illness, even the death of a child were experiences Alice shared with many of Arizona's pioneer women.

I first became acquainted with the stories of Arizona's pioneer women while working at the Sharlot Hall Museum in Prescott, Arizona. Tucked between the original Territorial Governor's Mansion and an authentically recreated ranch house is a small but stunning garden of old-fashioned roses. A bronze sign proclaims that this is the Territorial Women's Memorial Rose Garden.

The creation of a rose garden dedicated to Arizona's pioneer women was the idea of Dorothy McMullen. A historical garden, using native plants, had already been established on the museum grounds when McMullen announced her idea on June 14, 1949. With the help of a number of women's clubs—the Prescott Garden Club, the Alta Vista Garden Club, and the Yavapai Cowbelles—the memorial garden was well established and cared for by 1951. Originally, one rose bush was planted for each woman honored. With several hundred women now memorialized, the garden as a whole stands in their honor.

While the blooms are beautiful, it is the Rose Garden

archives, containing the biographies of each of the women honored, that is the real treasure. To look at the historical photograph of a woman in "gay nineties" puffed sleeves and to read about how this woman went alone to the far reaches of the county to teach school is to understand the realities of Territorial Arizona. The women honored in the Rose Garden were invaluable participants in shaping what was to become the State of Arizona. Suffragists, teachers, doctors, nurses, lawyers, ranchers, miners, artists, writers, wives, and mothers—they were pioneers all.

Arizona's pioneers include women who chose to defy traditional "women's roles." Women like Frances Willard Munds, president of the Arizona Equal Suffrage Organization, who became Arizona's first female legislator in 1914; Grace Sparks, secretary of the Yavapai County Chamber of Commerce in the 1920s and 1930s, whose influence on Prescott, Arizona, can be seen in everything from its buildings to its unique "hometown" atmosphere; and Sharlot Hall, museum founder and western writer.

While these women might be considered atypical, it should be remembered that all of Arizona's pioneer women were exceptional. Ranch wives and mothers were just as strong and independent as their more-recognized sisters. Mary Elizabeth Larremore Lange raised ten children, several of whom were born in a tent, on various ranches throughout Arizona. Catherine Cecilia Healy Bennett's love of children led her to care for five foster children in addition to her own four offspring. And Alice Donovan Curnow followed her husband from mining camp to farm to town, creating a loving sanctuary for her family in each desolate place. "How glad [I] was to be home again!" wrote Alice, returning home with her newborn daughter, of her little tent house with papered walls supported only by muslin and a floor covering of boxes and scrap lumber; "It was like camping out."

Living in harsh, isolated surroundings, Arizona's women blazed new trails, regardless of their occupations. These are the women, Arizona's territorial settlers, whom the Territorial Women's Memorial Rose Garden honors.

It was also at the Sharlot Hall Museum that I first met Mona Lange McCroskey. As the museum's research historian, she was responsible for collecting most of the oral histories held in the archives. We shared an interest in the stories of the pioneers, especially the women's stories. Like the women of an earlier era, she welcomed a newcomer into the community and shared valuable local knowledge with her. Soon, she was a friend and mentor.

It seems most appropriate that it is Mona who is retelling Alice's tale. It was through Mona's water rights research that Alice's memoir was discovered and her name added to the list of Rose Garden honorees. Mona is herself a product of intrepid Arizona pioneer women, including Mary Elizabeth Larremore Lange and Mona Denson Lange. As a result, she is uniquely qualified to interpret the events Alice relates. The unrelenting sun and the overwhelming heat, as well as the beauty of the desert in bloom, are all familiar. So, too, is the hope and interest with which Alice greets each new challenge.

Along with a practical understanding of the realities of life in rural Arizona, Mona adds an academic background in history with Bachelor's and Master's degrees from Arizona State University, as well as a Master's degree in library science from the University of Arizona. Her historical articles and photographic essays have appeared in the *Journal of Arizona History, Journal of the West, Smoke Signals,* and *Cactus & Pine,* the annual journal of the Sharlot Hall Museum. *Summer Sojourn to the Grand Canyon: the 1898 Diary of Zella Dysart,* a charming and subtly-edited account of a young girl's summer vacation, has received excellent reviews and is a favorite

with visitors to the Grand Canyon. For her exceptional contributions to historical research and western writing, Mona
was awarded the 2000 Sharlot Hall Award, which recognizes
those who have made valuable contributions to the understanding and awareness of Arizona and its history. It is
Mona's ability to turn files of dusty historical documents into
a lively narrative, where we readers can draw parallels
between our own lives and those of our pioneering ancestors,
which is her most appreciated achievement.

Historians Mary Logan Rothschild and Pamela Claire
Hronek, who conducted an oral history of Arizona women,
describe the ordinary woman as "not the first doctor or pro-
fessor or politician, but women who saw themselves as just
like their neighbors and probably less worthy of interview-
ing.[i]" Rothschild and Hronek, of course, quickly dispel any
notion that "ordinary" is anything less than laudable. Alice
Curnow must have felt the same in some way. Why else
would she have set her memories down in a permanent
form? Those of us who read her story will surely agree—hers
is a life both common and extraordinary.

Anne L. Foster
Archivist
University of Alaska Fairbanks

---

[i] Rothschild, Mary Logan and Pamela Claire Hronek. *Doing What the
     Day Brought: An Oral History of Arizona Women*. Tucson: University of
     Arizona Press, 1992. Pp. xiv.

Preface

Alice Jane Donovan was born in North Whitefield, Maine, on February 13, 1861, the second daughter of Edward and Sarah McNally Donovan. The Donovans were married in the Catholic Church in Whitefield on November 15, 1855. Edward, who was an engineer, left shortly thereafter to see the elephant. Sarah stayed in Maine where she gave birth to their first child, Mary, on September 28, 1856. Edward returned in April 1860 and remained in Maine until after Alice's birth. He then went back to California in December 1861, leaving his family in Maine. Apparently he believed his children would receive a better education in the East.

The Donovan family was reunited in Gold Hill, Nevada, in January 1877. Gold Hill was a part of Virginia City; if one lived north of "The Divide House" it was in Virginia City, if south it was in Gold Hill. Alice was sixteen years old and recalled that Mark Twain was writing a column for the *Virginia City Enterprise* when they arrived in Nevada.

Thomas W. Curnow was born "somewhere in northern Michigan" in 1855. He moved with his parents to Connecticut soon afterward. "Imbued with the pioneer spirit which settled the west," Tom went to Nevada in 1872 and began carrying silver bullion from the Comstock Mines in Virginia City to the United States Mint at Carson City. Alice Donovan met Tom Curnow in Nevada and they married in Carson City on December 18, 1879. She was eighteen; he was twenty-four.

With the decline of the silver boom in Nevada, Tom Curnow migrated to Globe, Arizona, arriving on January 6, 1881. His first employment there was as a butcher. He then worked as a blacksmith and tool dresser in the Richmond Basin silver district northeast of Globe. In 1883 Curnow went to work for the Old Dominion Mining Company, where he was head blacksmith for nine years, then master mechanic for seven years. He ventured into many other undertakings along the way. Alice followed him faithfully, often traveling in a wagon over the Pinal Mountains with a baby in her lap.

In 1896 the Curnow family moved to Mesa, in the Salt River Valley, with the intention of farming. However, with Tom's blacksmithing and mechanical expertise and his experience as a carpenter, it wasn't long until he opened and operated prosperous general repair shops in Mesa, and later, Tempe, Arizona. In Tempe Curnow was the agent for Pratt and Gilbert farm implements. The Curnows then relocated to San Diego in 1907, where Tom worked in the city sanitary department for three years. He established "an enthusiasm for the study of municipal sanitation which grew rather than diminished with the encroaching years."

When Curnow returned to Arizona in 1916, he became part owner of the Lower Miami Stage Company, ferrying miners between Miami and Globe. Alice came from California to join him in 1918. In 1924 he began serving on the Miami Town Council, where he was chairman of the sanitation committee for several terms. Alice Curnow was active in the Miami Women's Club and was installed as corresponding secretary on March 18, 1925.

When Tom's health failed, he and his wife returned to California and spent their declining years in Los Angeles. His death came in 1930; Alice followed him in 1940. They are interred in Forest Lawn Cemetery in Glendale, California.

Alice Curnow recorded her experiences in a retrospective narrative written between 1925 and 1940. While compiling the story she wrote to Sharlot Hall, Arizona's state historian, whom she admired very much:

The account of my experiences in Arizona will not, I am sure, be as thrilling as your own, especially as I came by train from Gold Hill, Nevada in 1881, coming into Casa Grande about 11:30 p.m. . . .

She was describing the last leg of her tiring trip from Gold Hill to Richmond Basin, Arizona, twenty miles north of Globe. The Curnows' reunion was the beginning of a lifetime together in Arizona as a territory, and after 1912 as a new state.

After her husband's death in 1930, Mrs. Curnow worked on her manuscript, "which was a blessing [because it] gave me something to do, after raising four children, then having Tom to care for in his helpless condition." She wrote, "So, if this is never published, it will have served a purpose."

Mrs. Curnow was a member of the Arizona Pioneers' Society in Tucson. In August 1940, nearing the end of her lifetime, she presented them with a copy of her 223-page manuscript, "The Journey With Tom." For more than sixty years it has been on the shelf at the Arizona Historical Society in Tucson, available to researchers and casual readers who happened across it. As the years go by, more and more authors are citing this typescript. The time has come to make Alice Curnow's story accessible as an important piece in the quilt of Arizona women's history. The original has been researched exhaustively and edited gently, with great respect and admiration for her pioneering spirit.

Mona Lange McCroskey
Prescott, Arizona
September 2003

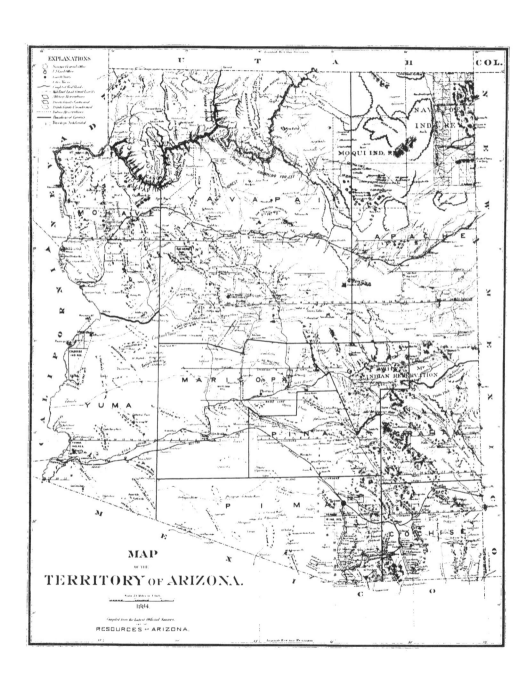

Chapter One

Through the window of the car, Alice Curnow watched the slender whirlwinds of sand rise from the desert floor and go spinning along over its surface. It seemed impossible that in so short a time there could be so great a change in temperature. That morning in Los Angeles the weather had been delightful and cool. In the afternoon of that same day the desert heat was almost unbearable to one coming from the High Sierras, as the train dropped down into the Mohave Desert.

At that time, in 1881, the Southern Pacific Railroad ran along the present site of the Salton Sea; where its waves now ebb and flow there were stretches of salt, white and glaring in the fierce sunshine. The heat beat down upon the car that was like a furnace as the train passed between drifts of sand.

Suddenly the train stopped. Alice wondered why, as no station was in sight. Nothing but endless drifts of sand. She tried to read, but couldn't sit still enough to see the words. She wet her handkerchief in water from the drinking fountain and bathed her face, but it burned worse from this treatment. Ice was provided, but that was before the day of electric fans, when one endured these discomforts as a matter of course.

"You all going t'be delayed [an] hour or so, mebby all night for all ah knows. T'heat dun spread t'rails," said the porter as he passed into the next car.

There were but three other passengers, all men, besides Mrs. Curnow, in that car, so that she had plenty of room to walk from one door to the other, trying to get a breath of air.

While the train had been in motion it had not been so bad, but to be still in that intense, glaring, suffocating heat was maddening. She thought of those who had crossed that sandy waste in wagons and wondered how any had survived the ordeal.

She returned to her seat, determined to take her mind off her discomfort, and [had] picked up a book when the porter came again, and as he quickly closed the windows, he explained, "We're suah going to have some san'storm. Just look at it coming."

He pointed to a dark, ominous-looking wall of whirling columns of sand reaching from the desert floor to the zenith and across the horizon. It was coming from the east and the setting sun gave it a dark, dreadful appearance. Alice's ears throbbed with the silence of the desert, which made the oncoming storm more fearsome. She was terrified, but fascinated, and [she] watched each drift of sand as the wind reached and curled its tip into the air. And always it came nearer.

Suddenly, with a roar, [the sandstorm] was upon the train, and although the windows were tightly closed, the sand sifted in, covering the windowsills, seats, and floor. The air was thick with sand. It was stinging Alice's lips, face, and hands. Her long, thick, dark brown hair that was moist from perspiration suddenly became stiff with sand. She could feel sand trickle down her body with her every movement.

The bell on the engine rang, and with a jerk the train started. It moved slowly and stopped, again and again. The porter explained the situation. "Sand drift moved up on th' track. Got t'shovel it off 'fore we can go on."

Men might be shoveling sand off the track, but Alice couldn't see the length of the car. Occasionally the train would move cautiously forward for short distances as the track was cleared, then stop. Night found it stalled and the sandstorm unabated.

The porter made up the berths and Mrs. Curnow lay down, but sleep was impossible. The heat was intense. When she changed her position, Alice could feel the sand falling off her face, that she had ceased to wipe, as that but increased her suffering.

At daybreak she went to the drinking fountain, to find that the ice had melted, and the alkaline taste of the water, which the ice had partly concealed, was worse than her thirst.

Day came, [revealing] nothing but sand. The storm was passing, however. At intervals the sun could be faintly outlined, and presently the train slowly resumed its journey, gaining speed where the wind had swept the track clear of obstacles, then passing slowly when another drift of sand was encountered. Going in the opposite direction from that in which the storm was traveling, the train soon passed out of it.

The sand had been rolled and curled beneath the violent blasts of the wind until its dunes were shaped like great snowdrifts after the wind has swept their sides into tiny

Casa Grande, near depot, 1892. *Arizona Historical Society/Tucson, #771.*

ridges. In places these dunes were higher than the train. It was a monotonous journey, riding slowly between hills of sand, stopping in sheltered places for the shovelers to do their work.

It was past midnight when the train stopped at Casa Grande. The porter helped Mrs. Curnow off with her baggage, and the train sped on its way. The few other passengers who had alighted seemed to have melted into the night, leaving her alone on the platform.

The agent was locking the door of the baggage room when she asked, "Will you please direct me to the hotel?"

He pointed down the track, across the road to an adobe building that loomed above the outlines of other little houses, saying, "Right over there, Miss."

Following his directions, Alice stumbled along the track until she reached the hotel, which consisted of a number of little detached houses, each about eight feet square. A knock brought the proprietor to the door, and with a lantern he conducted her across the extensive, brush-covered yard to one of [the small houses].

As he stepped inside he turned to her, saying, "Look out that you step high, that sill is five inches up."

"Why do you have it so high?"

"To keep out the water of the Gila River when it overflows its banks, and that's pretty near every time it rains."

He placed her baggage on the dirt floor, lighted a candle on a chair without a back at the head of the bed, and withdrew from the room.

Alice closed and locked the door. She noticed a curtain hanging from a shelf that was of the same shade as the adobe walls that were in their natural color. There was no ceiling under the dirt roof. [There was a] small window opening with small round sticks, set when the adobe was soft. The sticks were then immovable, reminding her of the bars of a prison. There must have been a similar opening in the rear of the building that faced the back of hers, for she could distinctly hear the conversation.

One would say, "Here! If you're going to play, ante!"

"It's your deal, Ned. Hell! If you're going to play seven-up, deal. Don't hold up the game."

"Come on," shouted another. "Have a drink on Sam! He lost."

"The hell I did. Frank lost it hisself, so he's inviting you all up to the bar. Come on!"

As she listened, Alice sat down on the edge of the bed, from where she could easily have touched the opposite wall, and unhappily contemplated her surroundings. Suddenly she saw two fiery eyes looking at her from under the curtain behind the door. Rattlesnakes! Was her first thought, because before leaving home everyone spoke of them when Arizona was mentioned.

At that moment she heard her neighbor shout, "Lights out," after which all was quiet.

Alice was too stunned to move for a moment, then, closely watching the eyes of the reptile, she slowly drew her feet up on the bed. At first she could not stand upon them; her knees gave way. She remained quiet so as not to disturb the snake. Slowly she rose up on her feet. The eyes of the serpent followed her own. Alice wondered what she should do. It would be impossible go to through the window opening even if she could break the sticks, and the snake was between her and the door.

Suddenly she clutched the parasol that she had been holding [even] tighter and, leaning over, caught the curtain in its crook and pulled it back. A little black cat and her kittens! The poor creature was quite as frightened as Alice! Looking back, Alice thought it sounded quite foolish, but it was the most terrible fright she ever had. After that, sleep was impossible and she waited for daylight.

At the first sound of activity outside Alice cautiously opened the door and looked down the narrow passageway between the two rows of little houses like her own. All of them seemed to be occupied; all the doors had been left open; [and] no one except herself seemed to fear intruders.

In the largest of the buildings Alice found Mrs. Fryer, the landlady. She was a hard-looking woman of forty or forty-five years. She was washing a tiny baby before a smoking fireplace. The poor little thing was blue with the cold. Mrs. Fryer explained that it was an adopted child and was eight months old. From its appearance Alice had judged its age to be about three weeks.

Pauline Cushman at Jere Fryer Hotel, Casa Grande, c. 1881. *Arizona Historical Society/Tucson, #50619, PC 122, Album A-1.*

As Mrs. Fryer flipped the baby over on its back upon her knee, it made no protest. It seemed too weak, and it drew up its little skinny legs and arms as tightly as it could. Its little chin was trembling and its eyes stared straight ahead, paying no attention to anything.

With the naked baby lying on her knee, Mrs. Fryer turned to Alice and said, "My husband is Jere Fryer. He was sheriff of this county. I am Major Pauline Cushman. I was

FRYER'S HOTEL,
CASA GRANDE, ARIZONA.

I am prepared to accommodate the traveling public with

Excellent Meals, and Clean, Comfortable Beds.

My New Rooms are Large, Well Furnished, and Quiet, insuring to
the Weary a Comfortable Night's Sleep.

Connected with the House is a

BAR, WELL SUPPLIED WITH GOOD LIQUORS AND CIGARS.

I ALSO HAVE A CORRAL AND FEED YARD, WHERE MAY BE FOUND THE BEST OF
HAY AND GRAIN.

JERE FRYER, Proprietor.

Advertisement for Fryer's Hotel, Casa Grande. *Arizona Business Directory & Gazetteer, Disturnell, 1881.*

a spy in the Union Army and for my work I received my commission from President Lincoln."

Alice wanted to cry out to her to cover the baby, but she was a woman whom one knew would take no suggestions from anyone, and it might be worse for the baby to interfere.

With the child hanging over her arm, Mrs. Fryer walked to a table across the room. Picking up a book, she said, "This is the story of my life. You may have it for a dollar and a half."

At that moment a man came to the door and announced, "The stage is ready."

Alice was glad to escape from Mrs. Fryer. ([Years] later, in a San Francisco paper, she saw an account of this woman's death, with an outline of her life in which it was stated that she was a commissioned officer under President Lincoln.)

ARIZONA STAGE COMPANY.

WM. H. SUTHERLAND,
SUPERINTENDENT.

JOHN C. LOSS,
AGENT.

Run a Line of Coaches from

CASA GRANDE

S. P. R. R.

VIA FLORENCE AND RIVERSIDE, TO

GLOBE CITY

Carrying U. S. Mail and Wells, Fargo & Co's Express.

Also, run a Daily Line of Concord Coaches from

FLORENCE,

VIA PINAL, TO

SILVER KING,

Carrying U. S. Mail and Wells, Fargo & Co's Express.

WM. H. SUTHERLAND,
Superintendent.

Arizona Stage Co. advertisement. *Arizona Business Directory & Gazetteer, Disturnell, 1881.*

[*Ed. In Casa Grande, Mrs. Curnow boarded a stagecoach belonging to The Arizona Stage Company for the trip to Globe, via Florence and Riverside. From Florence the 1878 freight road went across the Gila River, through Kelvin, over the mountain to Dripping Springs, by the El Capitan Mine, and around the east end of the Pinal Mountains to Globe.*]

It was very cool when the stage left Casa Grande that morning, but that condition was soon remedied as the sun rose from the desert horizon. Its first beams sent a premonition through Alice of the heat that was to follow.

A few miles out from the station the driver stopped the stage to call the passengers' attention to the Casa Grande Ruins.

"You see that little opening in the center room, half-way up the building? Well, that's the only opening into that room that is no more than six or eight feet square. I never saw it myself, but that's what I've heard. There's no stairs or steps of any kind. Must have been a prison, some folks think.

"Looks just like the picture that some man drew of it, two or three hundred years ago when the Spaniards were here, so a fellow that reads a good deal told me. All I know is that they made mighty fine adobe, whoever built that house, 'cause if you left an adobe house without a roof now, the way they make adobe, it would melt down into the ground in a year or two."

"Well, where did the people go that built this house?" one of the passengers asked.

"Nobody knows. Some think that a Gila River flood must have drowned them. They call this the lake. It has rained for a few days and that's the only time there is any water in this lake, just after a rain," the driver explained, as the stage traveled over a rise of ground and down into a few inches of water, through which the horses trotted, then up over another rise of ground into the silt dust of that road.

"Y'know, this Casa Grande and this lake interests me," the driver continued. "The fellow that told me about that room in that ruin, he told me that he thought this lake was a reservoir for the people that used to live in the 'Big House.'"

Clouds of fine dust were thrown into the stage with every revolution of the wheels, as it bumped along. At noon the stage stopped at the adobe hotel [Lewis House] in Florence, where the passengers took dinner.

Above the long dining tables were equally long strips of wide cardboard hanging from the ceiling, with a fringe of paper pasted across the bottom. From the center of these improvised fans, ropes were fastened with which Mexican boys swung them to and fro, to keep the air and flies in circulation while the meal was served. There were no screens, and the horses that were tied to hitching rails all along the dirt sidewalk drew flies.

On finishing dinner Mrs. Curnow returned to the stage, expecting to continue her journey. The driver asked, "Are you going to Silver King?"

"No. To Globe."

"Well, this stage is going to Silver King. It runs every day. The Globe stage runs from here only every other day, and this is the day it don't run."

Alice was terribly disappointed. Florence was such a disheartening place to stay! The houses were all adobe, with dirt roofs. Some were in their natural color and some were whitewashed, with the woodwork painted in various shades of blue. Many [of the houses] had adobe walls about five feet high around their yards, which [she thought] effectively kept out any faint breeze that might be stirring. These, too, were whitewashed and glared in the fierce sunlight.

[Mrs. Curnow observed that] Florence was the distributing point for the numerous mining ventures in that part of the country. It was in the midst of a rich agricultural region

Cottonwood trees along the Gila River, c. 1880. *Arizona Historical Society/ Tucson, #50192.*

where vineyards and peach orchards grew abundantly in the level fields. Cottonwood trees grew all along the bank of the Gila River north of town, and everything looked prosperous. But oh, the heat!

[Alice believed that] the time to be most homesick and lonely is to be a stranger in a town or city, and the larger the place; the more alone one can feel. That was her condition in that hotel with its whitewashed interior, where the white-wash was knocked off in spots, where no picture, not even a calendar, decorated its walls.

The room was long and narrow, with a very high ceiling in an effort to reduce the temperature, and the woodwork was painted a dark blue. Blue seemed to be the favorite color in Florence.

There was but one other guest in the hotel besides Alice: A very pretty, young woman with lovely golden-colored hair. Alice watched her, hoping that she would visit with her, but until late afternoon [the woman] had nothing to say. Then, as she walked nervously from one door to the other, she asked where Alice was going.

"To Globe," Mrs. Curnow answered.

"Oh, my dear! That's a terrible place to go. I have just come from there, where I was teaching school. The Indians would come into the schoolroom, sit on the floor with their backs to the door, and chatter until they got tired of watching me, and go away."

"Why did you go there?"

"I answered an advertisement in a San Francisco paper asking for someone to play the piano for a concert in Globe. When I got there they wanted me to play in a hurdy house where girls dance with men and get a percent on all the drinks they can persuade the men to buy.

"Of course, I wouldn't play in a place like that, so I got a chance to teach. That's where my husband, Hinson Thomas, found me, and we have just been married. You see, Mr. Thomas is Sheriff of Pinal County and that includes the Globe district. In his duty as sheriff he had to go there. I am certainly glad. Wait till you see him! He is the handsomest man you ever saw, and the best."

Again [the young woman] hurried to the door and back, clasping and unclasping her hands. She seemed quite distressed as she sat down beside Alice.

"There was a man killed just across the river from here, and Mr. Thomas has been gone ever since, looking for the murderer. I'm so worried, because he'll keep going until he gets the man, or perhaps the murderer will get him. I wish he would come. And now, may I ask why you are going to Globe?"

"My husband is there."

"What is his name? Perhaps I know him."

"Tom Curnow. I doubt if you know him as he has been there only since January 6th and has but just found work in Richmond Basin. Do you know where that is?"

"No, I don't, but it is only a little way from Globe. Where are you from?"

"Virginia, City, Nevada. The silver mines are closing there, so Tom wrote to George Newton, an old friend of his, to [find out] how things are in Globe and if he would advise Tom to go there. Newton answered promptly, telling Tom to come, that Globe was booming. Do you know Newton?"

"If he is a jeweler, I do. He fixed my watch for me."

"Yes, he is a jeweler. He lost his jewelry store in the great Virginia City, [Nevada], fire in 1875. Lost everything, and Tom let him have money to go to Globe, where he has prospered. So I am following Tom to Globe."

"Well, I hope you will like it better than I did."

"Is it worse than Florence?"

"Worse than Florence! My dear, Florence is a Paradise compared to Globe."

"Are the houses of adobe?"

"No. They are lumber shacks, usually of one or two rooms. And rent, if you can find a house to rent, is very high."

At that moment a horseman stopped at the gate and [Mrs. Thomas] hurried to meet him. Alice quite agreed with her that Hinson Thomas was a handsome man. [He was] dressed in Western style, with a broad brimmed hat, which was very becoming. As [the couple] entered the hotel, Alice heard him say, "He's in jail. He won't kill anyone else for a while."

❦

It was afternoon the next day when the Globe stage left Florence. An elderly [mining] man [named] Kennedy and a very serious young man were Alice's only fellow passengers. Mr. Kennedy was very kind and thoughtful, calling her attention to anything of interest along the way.

"You see that mountain on our left that rises straight up from the desert floor?" Mr. Kennedy asked. "Well, that is

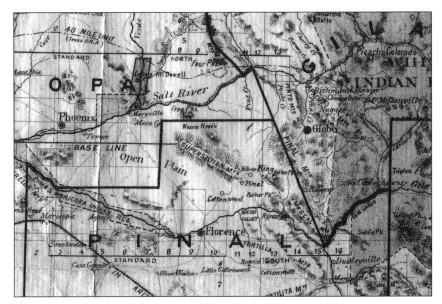

Map, Globe and vicinity, Arizona Territory, 1884. *Sharlot Hall Museum Library/Archives, Prescott, Arizona. Map Collection.*

Superstition Mountain. There is a legend that a tribe of Indians was driven by an enemy tribe over that cliff to their death, but I believe it's a white man's legend, as no man nor men could travel, much less fight, there. It is nothing but pinnacles of rocks and deep canyons its entire length.

"Every prospector in this country has tried to penetrate its vastness in search of a fabulously rich gold mine that the early Spanish explorers were supposed to have discovered, but none have succeeded in entering its fortress."

At the first stop for fresh horses, where the road ran through rolling hills and the dust of the desert had changed to the gravel of the hills, the mining man helped Alice out of the stage and they walked about to rest. He called her attention to the great variety of cactus growth.

"In the spring this is a wilderness of flowers. Every cactus you see will be in bloom. If it were three hours later you would hear why this is called Coyote Wells. The beasts seem to rise from the ground, as none are visible before dark. They give a weird cry, rather terrifying if one is not familiar with their habits. They never attack one.

"You may have heard of the empty desert, but at night millions of tiny creatures come from their hiding places in search of food. Last week I was crossing from Phoenix at night, to escape the heat, and the horses frequently jumped aside or backed in terror as a rattlesnake disputed their right-of-way."

The other passenger had not joined them or shared in any information given by [Kennedy]. He stood near the stage looking anxiously about him, as the country they were entering looked very forbidding. Alice noted that the name given in her mother's geography book to this part of the country was "The Unknown Region."

[The next stop was] Riverside. A poetic name, which Alice had pictured [as] a little settlement on the bank of a stream, [which in reality] was one adobe building with a dirt floor. Meals consisting of bacon, biscuits, and coffee were served to the passengers. It was also the post office for that part of the country.

Alice was sorry when the mining man left the stage at Riverside, explaining, "I have what I think is a very rich gold mine in this vicinity, and if I strike it as rich as I expect, I will ride over the mountain someday to see how you are making it."

Alice thanked him and waved her hand as the stage started that night at ten o'clock. It was as dark as it ever gets in Arizona, when there is no moon. [She could] always see about in the clear starlight.

When the horses plunged into the river, Alice screamed out in fright. The stage driver stopped to explain, "This here river goes way back east som'wheres and they ain't a bridge the hull way. This is the way we always cross it, and they ain't a mite of danger."

As the horses climbed up the bank out of the river the [remaining] passenger was thrown against Alice. He apologized, and then pompously announced, "I am on my way to Globe to learn what the prospects are there for opening a bank. Banking is my business."

This did not call for a reply, and there was no further conversation.

It was past twelve o'clock that night when the stage came to the top of a long hill and the driver, Andy [Hall], stopped his team to rest the horses. The sound of many horses and the rattle of [an approaching] wagon could be plainly heard. Andy drove off the road and waited.

Suddenly the stage was surrounded with horsemen. One of them asked, "Is Mrs. Curnow aboard?"

Andy answered, "Yes."

"Good!" said the speaker. "Me and some of the boys and Tom Curnow has come to meet her."

Alice had been chilled with fright when she heard them asking for her, but on hearing that Tom was one of them, she got out of the stage and waited, not knowing from what direction he would come. He jumped from the stage in which he had been traveling, before it had stopped, and had her in his arms. She was weeping hysterically, while the cowboys looked the other way or busied themselves with horses and spurs.

"Don't cry, Alice. I know you must be tired, but try and hold up until we get to Globe." Tom tried to console her.

"It's not that I am so tired, but when these men came I thought we were being held up by stage robbers, and when they asked for me I thought that perhaps I was to be kidnapped."

"Don't you worry. There is no place in the world where good women are respected more than in Arizona. When the boys heard that you were coming, they came along with me so that you wouldn't be lonesome or frightened going through the mountains tonight—not that there is anything to fear. The boys didn't realize that they would frighten you. They have been riding since early morning, and if you are not too tired I wish you would meet them."

"I certainly will, if they have taken all this trouble for my sake."

Tom turned to George Newton, who was standing beside him. [There were also] a Jim Hicks, Dan and Hank, whose other names she had forgotten, and five or six other cowboys and friends of Newton who had come to escort Alice to Globe.

Andy then called out, "All aboard! Can't hold up the U.S. mail no longer for ceremony."

"Wait a minute, Andy," said Jim Hicks. "Lem'me have your lantern for a minute, so's the lady can see into the stage t'see where she's going t'set."

Jim took the lantern from Andy, and, holding it up to the door of the stage he saw the banker and said, "Partner, you set with your back to the driver so's the lady will have more room."

"I paid for this seat and I'm going to sit right here."

"Now that's just where you've misinformed yourself, 'cause you ain't going to ride inside 'tall. You just step up 'long side of Andy."

"I told you that I'm going to sit right here. I paid for this seat."

Jim slapped Hank on the back and they both roared with laughter. Then, becoming serious again, Jim said, "We don't care what you paid, but you air sure going to move. Hank, you help this gent to get out of the stage. Then we'll decide what we'll do with him. Might's well leave him here."

Hank, a tall cowboy and powerful as an ox, reached in and lifted the man out, asking, "Now, what'll we do with him, Jim?"

"Well, if we leave him here a coyote might pack him off. I seen one the other day get a big calf on his horns and pretty nigh get away with him if I hadn't of come erlong just then."

At that moment the weird howl of a coyote was heard a short distance from the stage. Another farther away immediately answered it. Then, from all directions came the prolonged cries of the beasts.

"Well, the coyotes is waiting to see what we're going to leave them, Jim."

"Yes. 'N'then too, the rattlesnakes is awful plentiful in these parts, one of them might get him. They get so big where it's so hot. Le's ast him what he'd like."

But the man was speechless and helpless with fright, and he made no objections when the cowboys suggested that they throw him on top of the stage. They led him around to the front of the stage, where Jim took his feet and Hank took his shoulders. They swung him a few times and the man found himself seated beside the driver, who again urged them to start.

"Wait a minute, Andy, we want to give this guy a li'l reminder of this trip. You hold the light, Andy, and Hank, you go 'long round to the other side of the stage, you bein' th'best shot. When I count three, you shoot at this guy's head as clost t'his head as you can. Try not to hit him. I'll shoot at the same time. All right, one-two-three!"

At the word but one shot could be heard, although two had been fired. The stranger had slumped down into the boot of the stage. Jim climbed aboard, removed the man's hat, and reported, "No damage done."

Alice was horrified. She shuddered as she turned to Tom and hid her face on his breast. He patted her shoulder and laughed softly, saying, "Don't worry. The boys wouldn't hurt him. They're just giving him a good scare because he didn't promptly give his seat to a lady."

The horses started on a gallop down the hill into Dripping Springs Valley. On either side Alice could see trees and brush. Occasionally a cow would go shambling[1] out of the road as the stage went bounding along. She thought "bounding" was the right word, as there had been no pretense at road building. [The brush was] merely cut away and the boulders removed that were too large for the stage to pass over, leaving holes to be filled by the vagaries of nature, or to remain holes.

During the night the horses were changed at Idaho Bill's. Water was piped from the hill back of Bill's large rambling house and orchard to a trough on the road outside his fence. This provided water for his great herds of cattle that roamed in Dripping Springs Valley.

The horses, being changed so frequently, were never tired, and they traveled at a gallop uphill and down. When they reached the bottom of a hill they stopped so suddenly that, if the Curnows had not braced themselves by putting their feet on the front seat, they would have been thrown into that seat more than once during the night. Then, just as suddenly, [they] started up the next hill and they were thrown back. [Alice observed that] this had one good effect: it kept them awake.

---

1   A shuffling gait.

Chapter Two

It was daylight when they reached the summit [of the Pinal Mountains]. It was covered with a heavy growth of forest and several inches of snow, for which Alice was unprepared. She thought that Arizona was hot throughout the Territory, and that was the reason she was wearing only a lightweight summer jacket.

When she got out of the stage she couldn't stand. Tom helped her to her feet, but for a moment she couldn't take a step. Besides being stiff from her long ride, she was thoroughly chilled.

Two men, followed by two big dogs, came running from a long cabin built of slabs, to take charge of changing the horses. But when they saw Alice hobbling along, one of them came and, taking her other arm, helped her to the cabin door. He called to a man who was stooping over a cook stove, trying to crowd more wood into the blazing fire. "Here, Dick, you have company."

A pleasant-looking old man, his face covered with a short red beard, looked up, and, reaching both hands to them in welcome, said, "Come in! Come in!"

With his arm still around her, and holding her hands to keep her from falling, Tom introduced Dick and asked, "Will you give her something to eat? You know it will be four o'clock before we get to Globe."

"Will I? Just watch me! But first have her lie down on this bunk nearest the stove."

Then, taking a blanket from another bunk, which Alice was sure the dogs had shared, Dick handed it to Tom, saying,

"Better wrap this around her feet while I get a cup of coffee to warm her up. I always make a big pot full and keep it hot so's the boys can have some anytime they want it."

[Alice remembered,] "Never before nor since has a bed given me such comfort as did that bunk! To stretch out full length under those blankets that were dirty and full of dog hairs, was an indescribable joy."

Alice watched the cook prepare her breakfast. First he scraped the scraps from two tin plates out the window opening with no glass, but a wooden shutter that would slide either way in a grove along the wall. Then he cleared the shelf by throwing scraps and empty cans out the same opening. Alice could hear them roll down the hill. Next [the cook] brought a grain sack and wiped the shelf that served as a table, and then wiped the stove with the same bag.

Dick cut several slices of bacon, which he fried in a pan. From a fruit can he poured pancake batter on the top of the stove, while he apologized for not having butter or canned milk. He poured plenty of boiling water over the tin cups and plates and turned them upside down to drain before serving Alice's breakfast on a box by the bedside, as she was still too weak to stand up. Tom ate at the shelf.

It was wonderful what that breakfast did for her! She could walk after her second cup of coffee, sweetened with syrup.

The horses were ready and the driver was anxious to go as Alice thanked Dick for his hospitality, and urged him to dine with the Curnows when he came to town.

Globe lies directly north of the highest part of the Pinal Mountains, so that it was necessary to travel many miles east on the south side of the mountains before finding a pass through which to build a road. From there the road passed over the southwestern corner of the San Carlos Indian Reservation. They then started down through the forest that covered the rolling hills on the north side of the Pinals.

20-mule team, Casa Grande to Silver King, c. 1878-1884. *Arizona Historical Society/Tucson, #719.*

The forest extended down into the foothills, where the fine old fragrant juniper and lovely mesquite trees with their feathery foliage spread their crooked branches over the brush that grew beneath them.

Under the brush, the grass and flowers grew and spread down and over the great valley that stretched far toward the east, where herds of cattle were feeding. These herds increased as the years passed, and their trails to water provided a ready passage for the rainwater, which cut deeper and deeper into the rich soil. What were cattle trails [became] deep gullies, down which the water rushed in torrents, leaving the hills and valleys dry and barren, and where few or no cattle are now [years later] to be seen.

[Alice found] the country beautiful, after the sagebrush and horned toads of Nevada. She exclaimed, "Why, Tom! I thought Arizona was a desert."

"Well, you have traveled through its desert, but Arizona can give you any kind of scenery. Wait till you see the sunsets. They are gorgeous."

"Are we near the reservation?"

"Very near. Just where the road turns sharply toward the west."

"Will there be many Indians there, and are they dangerous?"

"You will probably see none. The reservation covers a large territory, and this is not the part the Indians like. They prefer the mountains, where they lived before they were placed on the reservation."

Where the stage turned west [onto the freight road from Willcox], it was narrow and dusty, with deep ruts along which great freight wagons were hauled by from sixteen to twenty-four mules. All supplies for Globe, including coke for the smelter, were brought in this way from Willcox, on the Southern Pacific Railroad.

These freight teams made [the stage] journey more tedious and more uncomfortable, as the places wide enough to pass them were far apart. The Curnows rode in the dust raised by a team until one of these wide places was reached, and the teamster waited for them to pass.

[Alice recalled that when they arrived in 1881], the business section of Globe was but two short blocks long. Narrow

Advertisement for Pascoe's Restaurant, Globe, Arizona. *McKenney's Pacific Coast Directory 1886-1887.*

Broad Street, Globe, Arizona, c. 1880. *Arizona Historical Society/Tucson, #14983.*

sidewalks of rough boards followed the contour of the land. No attempt had been made to level the ground. In some places it sloped up; in others it sloped down. Occasionally a step was provided to meet this difficulty when the slope was too steep.

❧

After dinner at the Pascoe Restaurant, Tom casually asked, "Did I tell you that we must go on to Richmond Basin tonight?"

"Tonight!" Alice exclaimed. "How far is it?"

"About twenty miles."

"Can't we wait until tomorrow? I'm so tired."

"Sorry," Tom said, "but you see, the only conveyance to the Basin is old man Drew's buckboard, in which he carries the supplies for his boarding house. He was kind enough to let me take the buckboard to meet you, but I must be back there in the morning in time for breakfast, with coffee and other things that he must have."

"When do we start?"

"I thought it would be best to start at once, then you can sleep as long as you please in the morning. What do you say?"

"What can I say? If we must go I suppose that settles it."

"I hated to tell you before you had your dinner, I thought you might feel rested after you ate."

"I do, but I could stop here without hurting my feelings. There isn't any other place beyond Richmond Basin to which you would like to take me, is there?"

Tom put his arms around her, saying, "Too bad, but you see I just can't help myself."

"Oh, it's all right. I shall probably sleep for a week when I find a bed again."

"And I will bring you your meals."

It was dark when they left Globe, and they had a passenger. The mules [traveled] at a good gait down the Miami Valley. About eight miles from Globe and just before they started up the mountains, one of the hind wheels on the buckboard collapsed. Alice was glad then that they had the passenger along, as he at once offered to go back to Globe for another wheel.

The Curnows went back about a half-mile to the only ranch house in that part of the valley, where they waited for the wheel. It was near morning on March 17, 1881, when [they arrived at the Drew Boarding House in Richmond Basin] and Mr. and Mrs. Drew kindly got out of bed and lit a fire for their comfort, for it was bitterly cold.

Mrs. Curnow slept late the next morning, and woke to find her husband gone. The room in which she found herself was built into a hill, which came nearly up to the roof. There was just space enough for a small window near the roof that gave very little light. The room was furnished with a bed and a box, on which a tin washbowl and pitcher were placed. [There were] plenty of nails in the bare board walls, on some of which Tom's clothes were hung.

There was not another thing in that room. When Mrs. Drew told Alice that her furniture, consisting of a black walnut bedroom set and a library table, cost $280 to bring from Willcox on the Southern Pacific [and on] to the Basin by freight wagon, Alice didn't wonder that her bedroom furniture was scanty.

She washed in cold water, with red and white soap that made an excellent lather. When she complained that night to Tom that her face burned terribly, he said, "You've used too much of that soap. I forgot to tell you about it. Not fit to wash anything but a horse."

Alice went out for breakfast to the dining room that opened off her bedroom, and was no improvement on the latter. It was long and narrow, with one small window, for windows were scarce, too. The table of three boards, without cover of any kind, extended nearly the whole length of the room, leaving just space enough to pass at either end, with long benches over which one stepped to be seated.

There was no ceiling under the bare rafters. [There was] a wide, door-less opening into the kitchen where the Chinese cook received his orders from patrons without leaving the stove. [Alice thought] this really unnecessary, since all he had to do was place the food on the table. The menu never varied.

[The meal] consisted of a platter of thin, evil-tasting steak, cooked until it was like leather. This was passed around the table. [They were served] bread, coffee, condensed milk, and nearly always, sugar. Sometimes this was missing. Occasionally, [the menu included] boiled rice or stewed dried fruit. For this diet the Curnows paid nine dollars each, per week.

The only other guest at that breakfast was Bill Chilson. Bill was not only late, but he was tired. Both arms rested their full length upon the table, from which Bill never lifted them. He didn't raise things to his mouth; he stooped over and moved his mouth from one hand to the other. He reached around his plate, too, without moving his elbows. Eating without exertion had become an art with Bill.

Alice watched him with interest, to see if he wouldn't forget sometime and move his elbows, but he did not during the entire meal. She thought, what a comfort a pillow would be to Bill. He was dirty, too, with his hair uncombed and his face unshaven.

After he had inhaled his second cup of vile coffee, Chilson informed Alice, "I and my two brothers found this camp. We drove the first wagon that ever come into Richmond Basin and picked up $82,000 in silver nuggets on top of the ground. That's why we called the mine 'The Nugget.' Gyp, he's my oldest brother, he went to Anaheim and bought a lovely home for my folks. Here 'tis, a picture of it."

Alice felt like assisting Bill as he raised one hand and, leaning heavily on the other, he took a photograph from his pocket. Holding it for her to see, he said, "You see, it's a fine two-story house in that orange grove, and you see that girl in the swell buggy driving that fast horse? Well, she's my sister."

Alice wondered how Chilson knew the horse was fast, as the animal gave no indication of speed as it stood to have its picture taken.

"Where is this mine of yours?" she asked him, having visions of herself picking up silver nuggets. If anyone as lazy as Bill could do so, Alice was sure she could carry a few.

"That's just it. It ain't."

"What do you mean 'it ain't?' Didn't you have this mine, or did you dream all this?"

"Well, you see, it's just like this. Gyp, he's my oldest brother; he went east and incorporated The Nugget and sold stock. He must of splurged a lot, 'cause when he got back he was nigh broke.

"He got E.F. Kellner—Kellner, he's got a big store in Globe and a lot of branch stores in all the little camps—well, Kellner, he put up for Gyp. He furnished the lumber for the mine and this house and all the supplies for both, you see."

Bill got heavily to his feet and, going to the door, he pointed to The Nugget. "They're closing it down," he said sadly. "Never got a bit of ore under the ground. Now, ain't that strange?

"Well, if the mine is closing, [I] wonder what we are doing up here?"

"You're all right. Tom never did work for The Nugget. You see, the Mack Morris [Mine] is further up the canyon, and they found ore under the ground. Same kind of ore. Looks for the world like taffy candy when you pull it out and wind the end round."

[Chilson pulled a silver nugget out of his pocket.] "Look at this! It's all I've got out of The Nugget Mine, and I'm always going to keep it. I bet if Gyp knew I had this, he'd want that, too."

Bill Chilson was a pathetic figure as he slouched out of the door, and without again looking at The Nugget he went off to his dugout home, a hopeless old man, although young in years.

⁕

After breakfast, Mrs. Drew invited Alice to go for a walk with her to gather wildflowers, of which there was a profusion all over the hills. Mrs. Drew was quite as despondent as Bill Chilson had been.

"If we had only stayed in New York," she said, "But Gyp Chilson told us such wild tales of wealth out here that Mr. Drew resigned his good position in a warehouse and joined Chilson in this venture. Here we are without a cent and Katie (her daughter, eleven years old) needing schooling. I don't know where to turn."

Alice was beginning to wonder which way would be *their* way to turn.

When Tom Curnow came for dinner at noon he was jubilant, saying, "I've got a job!"

Alice was astonished! "Didn't you have a job? What do you mean?"

"Well, I didn't want to tell you until I had to. I was working for Jim Hazard, who has a big butcher shop in town. I was put in charge of his branch shop up here. Jim never employs a married man. I didn't know this when I sent for you, and when I told Jim that you were coming, he discharged me.

"You were on your way then, so there was no help for it. I have been at the Mack Morris Mine every morning when the men were going to work, and this morning Tom West put me on sorting ore. Not much pay, $2.50 a day, but it's a start."

Tom ate his dinner with a relish that surprised Alice. That day she made a dinner of stewed dried apples. She mentally made a note that, after they had paid all of Tom's wages for their board, they would still owe Mrs. Drew two dollars at the end of the month.

Silver King, Arizona, c. 1882. *Arizona Historical Society/Tucson, #74162.*

Silver King Hotel, 1879. *Arizona Historical Society/Tucson, #51449.*

A week later Tom came home to dinner, again very happy. "Got a raise already," he said. "Going to work in the blacksmith shop in the morning at four dollars a day."

And he pressed Alice to him in his happiness as she sat beside him on the bench. She shared his joy. Now they would have a home of their own where they could have something to eat besides thin steak and muddy coffee.

That afternoon Alice walked all over the place, looking for a [site to build a] house. From the narrow road through the hills, Richmond Basin opens into a pleasant, grass and flower covered little valley that slopes gently up the hill to the foot of Twin Peaks. [The Peaks] rise abruptly to a great height, from which a range of mountains extends along the south side of the Basin. At the base of this mountain were the two mines and their boarding houses.

Across the slightly undulating land on the north side of the Basin, the store stood with a saloon on each side, built very close together. The builders hoped they would be the nucleus around which the future great city would rise. Not a house was to be seen, except the mining buildings, a grocery store, and the saloons. Not a very encouraging outlook.

She couldn't get used to the food. [Alice's opinion was that] it would have been excellent for one trying to reduce, as it removed all desire to eat. She again confined herself to stewed dried apples. She hadn't cared for them since!

"What's the matter, Alice, can't you eat anything?" Tom asked her anxiously.

"No. I am really not hungry. I will be all right in a few days, after I get rested and used to a bed again."

On rising from the table, Tom said, "Let us take a walk, I have something to show you."

At the foot of one of the two highest peaks of the Apache Range, they stopped and Tom asked, "Wouldn't this be a good place to build our home?"

"Our home!" Alice exclaimed. "Where's the lumber to build it?"

"I'll find it and tomorrow night, we'll begin to build right here. [Our house] will face down the hill and be near Tom West's. That will give you company and close neighbors."

Tom's material [the] next night was a number of trees from the hill above them. "These," he told Alice, "are the posts, and Dutchie [a man who worked with Tom] is going to help me dig the holes for them. I sent to town for canvas for the sides, but the roof isn't planned yet. That will come later."

"Let's begin now," Alice said, picking up the shovel that Tom had brought with him. But she could make no impression on the hard ground.

"Hold on. This house begins with a pick," he said as he marked its outline in the dirt. He dug a hole, and then set a post. Alice held it in place while he filled the hole with dirt and tamped it solid.

The Curnows were still staying with Mr. and Mrs. Drew, who were preparing to move to town, when Tom came in to dinner, saying, "Good news! The mining company is going to let me have enough lumber and shingles for a roof. Going to deliver it, too. How is that for luck? Glad I didn't waste any time planning a dirt one."

"Well, I'm surely glad we won't have one. Today the bugs and dirt were dropping all the time in that dugout at the foot of this hill. Did a woman ever live in it?"

Tom replied, "I don't know. But why did you go down to that dugout?"

"I wanted to know what kind of a home a dugout would make."

"I wouldn't go too far from the mine when you go for a walk. You know the Indians are about. Well, now, talking about dugouts, you won't mind having a dugout kitchen, will you?"

"Certainly not. That's the only kind I would consent to have."

They both laughed at the silly question. Alice knew just how hard it had been to drag those trees from the hills, and she was beginning to wonder if she would have to cook on a campfire.

With Dutchie's help, the house was soon finished.

"What will we do for a bedstead?" Alice asked, as the last nail was driven in the door made from scraps of lumber for a frame, with canvas stretched over it.

Tom was standing in the middle of the room, with a saw in one hand and a hammer in the other, looking over his handiwork. "If I can make a house out of nothing, I can certainly make a bedstead of the same material."

He picked up a piece of board about a foot square and, nailing a block of wood on the middle of this, he fastened legs on the block at an angle to prevent it from falling easily.

Presenting it to Alice, he said, "Here, Mrs. Curnow, have a chair."

"I'm glad you named it. I was wondering what it was for." She sat down on the chair, but it was not very comfortable and as she stood up, the stool fell over.

Tom laughed. He was happy. He was creating something. [Alice believed that] whether a stool or a cathedral, a dress or a statue, true happiness comes from creating something.

"Now, the bedstead. Where do you want it? For it's going to be immovable."

"In this corner next to the door, but are you going to make it with a pick?" Alice asked, as Tom stood with one in his hand. He didn't answer her, but dug a hole in the dirt floor and set a post in it, opposite the wall post. She began to think that her husband could build anything with a pick and a post.

From this he fastened pieces of lumber to the wall posts, from the foot of the bed, and from one wall post to another at the head. Over these Tom stretched canvas, and the bedstead was ready.

If only we could have a floor, Alice thought.

"We should be in here tomorrow night if the things come from town," Tom said as he locked the door, although there was nothing in the house.

Their things did come from town the next day, the driver complaining, "I had a time to keep that stove and the dishes from falling off the buckboard coming up the mountain."

After the stove was set up, the dishes [were placed on top of] the trunk in the corner. Alice had to remove them every time they needed clothes, as the trunk was the only place they had for them. The Curnows were ready to go housekeeping.

❧

Alice was busy washing one morning, and trying to

keep the tub on the "milking stools"—there were but two, so they had to be nicely balanced or the tub would tip off— when a man carrying a legal-looking black book came to the door, saying, "I am the assessor. The Horrel family in Miami Valley has become so numerous that they demand a school- house, so for this"—he looked about the Curnows' house and furniture, "h-m-m-m-m, I shall assess you twenty dollars."

And that was their first donation to education in Arizona. That day Alice was certainly glad that her freight had not arrived, although she had been so anxiously wishing it would come. If it had, she doubted if they could have paid the assessment!

The "milking stools" were not very restful seats, so when Alice had finished her washing she lay down on the bed. After a few moments' quiet, she saw a lizard running up the canvas wall behind the stove. She was always afraid of crawlers, so [she] picked up the hatchet and threw it at the creature, thinking to frighten it away. Instead, she hit [the lizard], cutting off its tail. Alice believed that was the only time she hit what she aimed at!

Tom began at once on the dugout kitchen. He had it nearly finished when their freight came, but they didn't open the box until they would move into the kitchen. Tom was working on the dirt roof [for the kitchen], and Alice was driv- ing nails and digging shelves in the dirt wall for her cooking utensils, when she uncovered a centipede. She screamed for Tom. Alice held the centipede with the pick, and it swung itself around the handle from side to side in its efforts to escape. Its length of five or six inches increased to twice that length in its struggle.

At last they moved into the new kitchen, and although Alice had many lovely kitchens afterwards, none ever gave her the pleasure that one did.

"Going to have a treat today," Tom said as he sat down

for dinner. "The Chinaman is on his way up here with fresh vegetables."

"That will be a treat. Now if someone would milk a few of the cows that are running around these hills and give us something besides condensed milk, we would be well supplied."

"Not a chance in the world. Calves need the milk, so what cattleman would bother about people? They don't have milk or butter on their own tables. They are all here for money, and to a cattleman, calves represent just that: money."

⟡

Just after they moved in an Indian woman with a naked baby about four months old came to the door. The weather was bitterly cold. Alice had no children whose clothes she could give to [the woman], so she pinned a woolen basque[2] about the child. The next day the woman returned to show Alice that her baby was again naked and cold; Alice gave it up.

⟡

Alice Curnow was the fortunate possessor of a catalogue from Weinstock and Lubin of Sacramento, the first catalogue she had ever seen. She had heard that, to the early settlers of the prairie country, Montgomery Ward's catalogue was called "The Desert Bible," because it was studied so regularly. To Alice and Mrs. West, Weinstock and Lubin filled the same office.

They studied it together and separately. They knew everything in it. Mrs. West's choice was a blue velvet jacket; Alice's was a red velvet-covered trinket box. Alice would have sent for the box, except that she had no place to put it.

One day Mrs. West was very happy. Her father had

_____

2   A close-fitting bodice.

given her some extra money to spend, and she took Weinstock and Lubin home with her to make out her order. Later in the day Alice saw her going to the post office, carrying her baby, her two little boys running ahead of her.

The women frequently sent for little things, for Kellner's store didn't even carry thread. Mrs. West had always included her order in Alice's, and [the order] was always addressed to Mrs. Curnow. But this time Mrs. West had boldly given her own address, and had happily confided to Alice that she had ordered some shirts for her husband.

They couldn't expect her package before two weeks [had passed], but they did hope it would come earlier. Instead, it was two days past the time when Alice saw Mr. West coming from the post office, carrying a package.

Alice wanted so much to be present when that package was opened! She knew everything that should be in it, but she was most anxious to see the blue velvet jacket.

Mr. West was a harsh, tyrannical man whom Alice felt frowned on visitors, so she forced herself to wait until she felt sure that he had gone back to the mine. Then, running down to the Wests' back door, she was shocked to see him holding a shirt with his feet and tearing it to pieces, while he cursed and swore at [his wife] for sending for things, unless he said that she might do so.

Mrs. West was standing with her back against the wall, one hand behind her and the other arm across her eyes, as if she would shut out the sight of that madman. Alice didn't see the velvet jacket then, nor did she ever see it. Perhaps it went the way of the shirts.

Alice fled in terror from that maniac, and she did not go back when she saw him leaving. She didn't want to embarrass Mrs. West if she had been seen at the back door. While Alice was walking from one door to the other, Mrs. West came in her house.

Mrs. West was a slender, pretty little woman with the fair hair of her German ancestors. Her fair face that usually had a bit of color in it, was [now] quite gray, her eyes looked weary, and she stood with her arms hanging down as if she had no life left. When she looked at Alice, Alice knew that Mrs. West had seen her at the door.

Alice put her arms around Mrs. West, and she laid her head on Alice's shoulder, where she sobbed as if her heart would break. Alice stood without a word. What comfort could she give in such grief? She led Mrs. West to the bed, and they sat down together. Alice held her arm about Mrs. West until she had her cry out.

Then, drying her eyes, she said, "I hate him more every day. You don't know how cruel he has been to me. One time when we were living on his big cattle ranch in Idaho, which he still owns, the Sioux Indians were on the warpath. The officer sent a runner to tell us to come to the fort, but [Mr. West] told the runner he wasn't afraid.

"I was horribly frightened, but had to stay if he said so. I was just getting Charlie, my baby then, ready for bed when we heard them coming, whooping and yelling. I had sense enough to blow out the light. Then we ran into the brush a few hundred yards from the house that we watched them burn. I nursed the baby all the time, in fear that he might cry and they would find us. My husband was frightened then, and I was glad."

Mrs. West stayed with Alice for some time. Then, getting quiet, she smiled wanly. "Well, my little boys need their mother, so I will go back to them. You have been kind to me and it has helped."

That evening while eating supper, Tom remarked, "West has been cranky all the afternoon. Nothing nor nobody could suit him. I felt like throwing the hammer at him every time he came into the shop. There was nothing wrong; he just wanted to kick."

"You think there was nothing wrong? His wife bought some shirts for him without his permission and he tore them all to pieces. I think he's crazy."

"If he isn't he hasn't far to go."

Tom sat at the table smoking and looking at Alice rather anxiously, she thought.

"How are you feeling?" he asked Alice.

"All right."[3]

"Well, I was talking with some of the men who have families, and they all advise that you go home. [They feel] that it isn't safe for you to stay here."

"Don't be silly, Tom, there is plenty of time."

"No, there is not. If I could go with you it would be all right to wait, but later you will not be able to travel so well, and I am worried."

So Alice prepared for her journey, because in that day it was a *journey*.

---

3   Mrs. Curnow was pregnant. She does not talk much about any of her pregnancies; it was the Victorian Age and women did not mention their "delicate condition."

Chapter Three

When the couple came down out of the mountains to Globe, word had been sent from San Carlos that Geronimo was on the warpath. As the stage road ran through the reservation, Tom advised that Alice go over the Silver King Trail.

[*Ed. Sure-footed mules conveyed travelers over the Silver King Trail. They were the only animals that could navigate the rocky hillsides and the dangerous canyons. There were also daily express and freight mule trains, as this route required less time from the railroad to Globe, a distributing center for the outlying mines and ranches.*]

"But I have never been in a saddle in my life," Alice reminded her husband. It was sidesaddle, even in the West, in those days.

SILVER KING AND GLOBE
Express and Saddle Train.

ROBERT STEAD, - - PROPRIETOR.

Connecting at Silver King with the Coaches of the Arizona Stage Company.

This is the shortest and most comfortable route from the Southern Pacific Railroad to Globe. Particular attention given to the comfort of passengers.

FARE, - - - $5.00.

EXPRESS MATTER CARRIED AT REASONABLE RATES.

Silver King and Globe Express and Saddle Train advertisement. *Arizona Business Directory & Gazetteer, Disturnell, 1881.*

"That's nothing. It's just like sitting in a chair. A mule never travels fast. In fact, you will have trouble keeping him moving. You can't go by stage. The Indians might kill you. And I won't take you back to the Basin. Do you want to stay here?"

"No, I'll go by the [Silver] King Trail."

She traveled by surrey to Bloody Tanks, where the guides with mules were waiting. She managed to get on a mule. The guide said as he handed her the reins, "Just let him alone. He'll follow the leader."

But that mule must have known that Alice was not acquainted with mules, for he started off on a trot. When he was going up, she was always coming down, and for a few dreadful moments she thought that mule was playing ball with her, until the guides surrounded her. It was the only time the mule moved without protest for the rest of that day.

[After stopping] for a chicken dinner at the Iron Ranch on top of the mountains, Alice had difficulty getting on the mule again. So when they came to Devil's Canyon and the guide told everyone to walk, she insisted on remaining on the mule. She was afraid that she would be unable to remount. But when [they were] halfway up that terrible gorge, when every time the mule put his front feet on the rock above and gave himself a boost to the next level, and she looked down that awful chasm, Alice wished she had taken the guide's advice.

She managed to stay on the mule until they reached the summit. It was not far, then, to the end of the day's journey, where she stayed at the Williams Hotel in Silver King.

The next morning, Mrs. Williams, a young German bride, very strong and with no sympathy for weaklings, called Alice.

"The stage will leave in half an hour. You'd better get up now. They won't wait for you."

Alice rolled over, saying, "Oh, I can't travel today! I'm too sore to move."

"Get up. You're no worse than anyone else. You'll be all right after you move around."

And Alice got up. For a while she thought it would be impossible to go on, but when she looked at Mrs. Williams, she decided it would be better to try.

[From Silver King] four horses drew the stage. They galloped along until they reached the Gila River. The driver stopped and the passengers, all men but Mrs. Curnow, got out of the stage and into a boat. Alice was no more acquainted with boats than she had been with mules.

The driver asked, "Do you want to cross in the boat?"

"Isn't it safe in the stage?" Alice asked. She was thinking of what that *other* driver had told her: "This is the way we always cross, and there ain't a mite of danger." It was the same river, only in another place, she reasoned.

"Oh, yes, I suppose it's safe enough," replied the driver.

Alice, thinking they were giving her a choice of pleasures in crossing the river, remained in the stage. She often wondered that those men allowed her to take that danger.

The river was very wide there, and in the middle of the stream the water came up so high that she had to put her feet up on the seat, where the water lapped the edge. But she was not afraid because "This is the way we always cross" again came to her mind, and she had never seen a river in flood. That was the last time even a boat could cross the Gila River for five days!

It was August and the little town of Florence hadn't changed any. Mrs. Curnow was glad she didn't have to stay there another day, for the rain that was falling didn't improve the appearance of the place.

By the time she reached Casa Grande, the water of the Gila was flowing all over that country. Two trains, one going east and one going west, were stalled, with twenty miles of track between Tucson and Maricopa washed out

Alice stayed in that dreary little one-room house at [Fryer's Hotel] for three days, where even the little black cat would have been welcome, while the rain fell constantly and the river seemed to cover the earth.

To reach the waiting room, which was away from the buildings some distance, Alice had to wade in water over her ankles. She became so ill that a doctor was called.

The railroad company had to provide for the passengers while they were delayed, [waiting] for the railroad to be repaired. Supplies in Casa Grande were running low, so the work was being rushed.

On the third day word came from the station that the train would "pull out in a few minutes." What a relief! The train did pull out, until it came to a high place on the track, where it stopped for another day. The passengers were served salt pork and beans with crackers, the same fare provided for the Chinese railroad builders. They had to drink the water that was flowing across the country. It was not too well settled, and too warm to be palatable.

Alice thought of stories about the richness of the country bordering on the Nile, made so by the silt from the mountains carried down by that great river. Surely the Gila River had made this valley just as rich in the silt it had carried down through the ages, and they were having visible evidence of the silt.

Chinamen were passing in a continuous line, carrying railroad ties upon their shoulders. These they fastened in squares like corncob houses, then sank them one upon another until they reached the surface of the breaks in the railroad bed, through which the water was rushing. On these ["houses"] the rails were laid, over which the train would slowly pass.

Arizona may be a desert in dry weather, but when the Gila River [flooded], the country was covered with weeds. Alice noticed a tall, slender, rapid-growing one, upon every one of which she believed was a large, fat, black worm. They climbed rapidly up the whip-like arrow-weed until the weed began to bend over. Then, just as rapidly, they retreated to the water line, then climbed again, and again retreated.

[The worms] furnished amusement for the passengers, some of whom began betting on a worm, if it would reach the top or fall off and drown. One group became so interested in a race between two worms, betting on which would fall off first, that they borrowed lanterns from the trainmen to continue the watch after dark.

The train was behind schedule when they reached Sacramento. Mrs. Curnow went to bed thinking that she [would be awake when her train was to leave], so she left no word to be called at eight o'clock that night. When she awoke it was eleven, with another day to pass alone.

When she got home [to Virginia City, Nevada], she found her mother dreadfully frightened. She didn't know that Alice was coming, and she had just received a wire from Tom saying, "Alice left here ten days ago. Has she arrived home yet?"

Alice had been so ill that she hadn't sent word to Tom. She had been told that no mail would go through for several days, so there was no use in writing.

The Curnows' daughter, Alice, was born on February 14, 1882, [in Gold Hill, Nevada], the day after Mrs. Curnow turned twenty-one years old. She started back to Arizona when the child was two months old.

On the train Alice heard the passengers talking about General Crook being replaced by General Miles. Said one, "Well, now, perhaps we will get some action. Crook has never been a successful Indian fighter. He is always just too far behind them to be a protection to the settlers. I know, for I live in Tombstone, and we settlers have been demanding his removal for some time."

In Casa Grade a wire was waiting for Alice from Tom, telling her to return by way of Silver King, where he would meet her and carry the baby. "The Indians are again on the warpath," the message said.

Tom was waiting for his wife in Silver King, and he carried the baby with his arms straight out before him. Both Curnows were the youngest in their families, and they knew very little about babies. Alice believed his own was the first baby Tom had ever held in his arms.

When they got off the mules for dinner, Alice found her baby evenly striped red and white! She had covered her face with a veil to protect her from the sun, and the baby had gotten it pulled down from her eyes, and [she] made a fuss when her father put it back. Tom, thinking the baby would be more comfortable with her mouth uncovered, [left the veil off.] So with her chin, nose, and forehead covered by the veil and cap, and her mouth and eyes bare, she looked like one of Geronimo's warriors in war paint! Alice soothed her with lotion as best she could, but they had to go on.

Mrs. West was waiting to welcome the baby when the buckboard drew up to the Curnows' home. Tom proudly threw open the door.

Alice exclaimed, "Oh, isn't this lovely! How did you do it, Tom?"

"I lined it with unbleached muslin, and then papered over it. But, my dear, you will have to be careful not to lean against the unsupported decoration. [It's] just cloth between the posts."

"But the floor under the carpet, where did you get the lumber?"

"Boxes and scraps of lumber fitted together. [I] had lots of fun while you were away."

"Well, I thought we would never use that carpet. Doesn't it look lovely?"

"It does. But the mice had eaten a hole right through the other one. We should have opened it and looked it over once in a while, or given it to someone."

"And a rocking chair! Tom, how did you get it up here?"

"The brewery man has to come up twice a week to supply the two saloons here. He told me that he would bring the chair for the price of the beer it displaced. It displaced nine dollars worth of beer, but it's worth any price when you have to hold a baby.

"And look at this." He took an Indian blanket from an easy chair. "Made it myself. A box and a tree. Try it."

Alice did, and she found it very comfortable. Tom had fastened a limb from the lower front corner along the side of the box on the right angle for the back. This was braced with another limb up the back of the box. A gunnysack [was] fastened across the back, and with a pillow on the seat and an Indian blanket over it all, it made a lovely chair.

How glad Alice was to be home again! It was like camping out. Every afternoon through that summer they had a shower, and from the front of the house Alice had a wonderful [panoramic view] before her. They were high above the Miami Valley, over which they could see on the horizon the Pinal Mountains circling toward the north, where along its mountain peaks were stretches of sunshine, then thunderstorms moving along.

In the evening these storms were more spectacular. When two would meet the fireworks were stupendous. Alice watched the storms develop and pass away on the faraway peaks. First [there would be] a dull flash, and then quicker and brighter ones that passed into streaks of fire. Rising from a center, they flamed in all directions, like fiery snakes leaping and gliding into oblivion. To be in their midst would have been terrifying, but from their great height where they could see several of the [thunderstorms] rise and pass away, they looked as puny as a baby thrashing its hands in protest to life.

While Alice enjoyed watching the storms, Tom had his eye on the highest part of the Pinals toward the south. Numerous forest fires made that mountain look like a great city in the evening. Knocking the ashes from his pipe, and pointing with its stem, he said, "Look! Between the forest fires and three sawmills, that forest will soon be destroyed. When I was working for Jim Hazard, I took a load of meat up to Kellner's mills, and while the horses were eating I looked around at the destruction going on.

"Great pine and black walnut trees were cut down, leaving stumps as tall as the cutter. No one bothered to stoop [over to cut the trees close to the ground.] There were plenty of trees. Then, a yoke of oxen came pulling a great log through the young growth. Any young tree too big for the oxen to tramp down was cut down by the driver, who carried

Sawmill in the Pinal Mountains, 1880s. *Arizona Historical Society/Tucson, #91875.*

an axe for that purpose. The oxen tramped out any plant life that might remain.

"When the growth of God-knows-how-many years is destroyed, the sawmills are moved to a new section of virgin forest, where this method of destruction is repeated."

"What a lecture, Tom, but what about our house? Didn't you have to cut down trees to build it?"

"Don't be ridiculous in your comparisons. If everyone in the district built his house from the forest it wouldn't injure it, but that fire will, and I believe it is set to clear the way for the lumberman, else why were there no forest fires before we white men came here?" [*Ed. Of course, there were.*]

"Who owns the mills that you speak of?" Alice asked.

"E.F. Kellner, Jack Eaton, and a man named Breman, all working with the same disregard of the future. I love trees, and I am going to plant them wherever we live. Then one can be my monument."

One afternoon the weather was delightful after a few days of rain that had been extensive over the country. The women and children of the camp climbed to the top of the hill directly behind the Curnows' house. The hill was a shoulder on the northernmost of the Twin Peaks, whose top was about halfway to the summit.

For some distance they followed the trail to the mining camp of McMillan, which was six miles over the mountain to the east of Richmond Basin, on the edge of the Indian reservation.

Leaving the trail, the climb became more difficult, especially as they neared the top, which was covered with small black rocks, flat and smooth on both sides, and of uniform thickness of about three-fourths of an inch.

It was two steps forward and one back, as the rocks had no foundation and slipped easily. But the wonderful view from the summit paid for the climb!

On the south and east, high mountains towered above the climbers, but toward the west and the north and far below them, there was a vast sea of mountain peaks, without a visible level spot.

The recent rains had cleared the atmosphere, so that each peak stood out clearly and distinctly. A few fleecy clouds at the end of the storm floated lazily above them, sometimes encircling the higher [peaks] like collars. The Salt River looked like a silver ribbon winding along between the hills.

As the afternoon lengthened, the peaks toward the north took on various shades of yellow, purple, and gray; toward the west a golden shade predominated. There were no red barns nor trim white houses with green blinds, nor horses with harness or traces to take nature's beauty from the scene, and from where Mrs. Curnow sat, the houses of the camp were out of sight. [There was] nothing but the vastness and silence of an Arizona landscape that was very impressive. Even the children were quiet.

The descent from the hill was quite as difficult as the climb had been. The whole hillside of rocks moved with them, gaining in speed until the McMillan Trail at the bottom of the canyon checked their flight.

At dinner that evening Tom asked, "Tired after your climb?"

"Yes, and I will be black and blue from the rocks I encountered on my way down. Did you ever notice the formation of those rocks on the top of that hill? They don't seem to be a part of the ground up there."

"Yes, I did, when I was on my way to McMillan one time. They remind me of an old slag dump when it is breaking up."

"What is a slag dump?"

"The waste from a smelter."

"Tell me about it."

"Well, the ore is mixed with inflammable material, such as coke, and lime. This is put into the jacket where the fire is already burning, and with the help of an air compressor that is sending in a mighty blast (something like the early settlers used a bellows in the fireplace to make the fire burn), the ore is reduced to a liquid state.

"When it has reached the right consistency, a man with a long steel bar digs out the earthen plug and the slag flows out into a large iron pot on wheels. When the slag pot is full, the man with the steel bar drives in another mud plug, which immediately hardens and stops the flow.

"The pot of slag is then wheeled away and tipped over, and spreads in a thin layer. Time breaks it up in small pieces, but they will be of even thickness."

"But what connection has the slag with these rocks?"

"Well, I thought that perhaps in prehistoric times a volcano might have thrown them out."

"That's an idea! And it would explain why the silver nuggets were found only in one place. From Miami Valley the Twin Peaks look to me like a gigantic chair. The Twin Peaks are the high back and the Basin looks like the seat. Where do you think the volcano was, Tom?"

"Between the Peaks. Might have sunk in that low place between them and closed the mouth."

One evening Tom was reading. "Alice, here is *The Police Gazette*. See if you can find your picture in it," he said as he handed the paper to her.

"My picture in *The Police Gazette*?" she asked. "What do you mean?" All the time she was examining the paper Tom was washing up.

"Right here," he said, pointing to a picture.

"Remember the dance you attended when Mat Canavan was superintendent of the New York Mine in Gold Hill, Nevada, and he had a dance floor laid at the thousand-foot level? Well, there is an account of the affair with a picture of Mat Canavan and his wife leading the grand march. Doesn't look much like Canavan, does it?"

"No, indeed. Will I ever forget it? The heat was dreadful, and when we couldn't stand it any longer we were invited to the carpenter shop, where a sumptuous banquet was served from the carpenter's bench, on tin plates. Champagne was drunk from tin cups, just as the miners were served in earlier days."

"There was plenty of champagne, and Mr. Jessup, Mrs. Canavan's music teacher, drank so much that he was pouring cupfuls of liquor into his coat pocket!"

"After the banquet we were invited to Mr. Canavan's home where we enjoyed a musical entertainment."

༒

Tom seemed absent-minded one night. Alice knew he was worried about something, and as they were preparing for bed, she asked, "How are you and West getting along?"

"If we don't get along better than we have been, you and I will be moving."

"What! After fixing up the house like this?"

"This house wouldn't keep me. I left Nevada for less than Tom West has done to me."

"What has he done?"

"I have been working on an invention in machinery for some time. A couple of months ago Baldwin, the general manager of the mine and mill, was here, and West called me to explain my ideas to him. I knew at once that West had made Baldwin think that it was his plan, but he was too stupid about machinery to explain how it worked.

"All he knows is cattle raising. That's all right, but why doesn't he stick to cattle raising? He got this job through his friends, for he knows no more about mining than he does about machinery.

"Baldwin was very much interested. He told me to drop everything, get all the help I needed, finish it at once, and send it to him. He said that if it worked as well as I expected it to that he would have it patented.

"West interfered with me in every way he could. Materials disappeared, patterns were misplaced, and if I wanted a particular helper he was always needed someplace else, until I told him that I would finish it at home after work and patent it myself.

"He apologized, saying that things in the mine had not been going so well, and he had been bothered. After that, I should have everything I wanted. I finished the model; it worked fine; and I turned it over to West to send to Baldwin. Now I am waiting for a report. I believe West has had one, for he is getting insolent again."

"But can't you have the thing patented yourself?"

"Not much chance for a poor man to buck a company, so I'll forget it."

Alice changed the subject. "You haven't told me about the Indian scare you had while I was away."

"The women and children went to town. Mrs. West has a very interesting story to tell you about her experience there. But here, West ordered a bulkhead built around the machinery of the mine. We built it according to his orders and then went across the canyon, shot at it with government rifles, and the shots went right through!

"After that we just went into the mine at night. Not a bit of danger. The Government sent rifles and ammunition, and from the tests we made on the bulkhead, their shots were very penetrating.

"As you know, the Indians did not come on this side of the mountains. They went through McMillan."

"I hope they never will come on this side."

❦

It was one of those days when everything goes wrong: In her hurry Alice had even spilled some dirty water into the bucketful that Tom had to carry from the mine. It was nearly noon before she found time to sweep the dirt from her back door, that she had to leave when the baby cried.

Intent on her work, Alice was startled to find a tall Indian youth standing beside her, with nothing on but a g-string. Holding a mockingbird toward her, he said, (or so she thought) "Uhn-hun-ah-hueh-ha-chee?"

Alice must have shown her alarm for, coming a step nearer, in a threatening manner [the Indian] made her understand in sign language that he wanted to sell the bird for one dollar.

Alice shook her head and motioned for him to let the bird fly away. His eyes blazed as he raised his hand above his head and threw the bird at her feet, so hard that the little thing was killed.

Enraged at the sight of his cruelty, and without stopping to think, she raised her broom to strike [the Indian]. He turned and fled, and Alice chased him down the hill. Suddenly she stopped, aghast at the thought of what she would have done if he had turned on her. But he didn't turn; he was still running when he passed from sight into a canyon.

Alice had just returned to the house when Tom came in for dinner. He picked up the baby and played with her for a few minutes. Then as he turned to the washstand, he said, "We had quite an exciting time at the mine this morning. The engineer was repairing the engine and had taken the cable off, leaving it coiled on the ground with the other end hanging into the shaft.

"In some way this end of the cable started into the mine, and Mr. West, thinking he could stop it, jumped into the middle of the coil. To our horror, he was being dragged to the mouth of the shaft when the cable flipped about his leg, breaking it, and [the cable] disappeared, leaving him on the edge of the shaft. It was all done so quickly, no one had a chance to move."

As he hung up the towel Tom turned to Alice and said, "What's the matter, Alice, are you sick? You are as white as death."

"No, only nearly scared to death. With a broom I chased an Indian clear off the hill." She told Tom all about it, and with a hand on each of her shoulders, he looked anxiously into her face.

"Alice, that was dangerous. Besides, the buckboard just came in and the driver brings word of another Indian uprising. This fellow may attack you when you won't have your broom. Dear, I am frightened for you."

"Well, it can't be helped now, and I will watch for him this afternoon until you come home," Alice said.

"No, I can't leave you here. Take the baby and come to the mine with me."

Alice spent a very pleasant afternoon. Tom made her comfortable in an office chair, and another for the baby, for which she had brought pillows. Mother and child were placed right on the edge of a canyon beside the mine, where trees and brush grew abundantly, and in the bottom of the canyon a little stream of water trickled musically over the rocks.

Alice watched a pair of brilliantly colored red birds with handsome topknots hop about in the bushes. Occasionally a large blue bird came hopping through, but didn't join the red birds. Then a dark gray bird showing a few white feathers flew like an arrow to the topmost branch of a tall tree. As it lit, its tail was raised at right angles to its body. Then, as it balanced itself, it broke into song. Alice didn't need anyone to tell her it was a mockingbird. It didn't need beautiful plumage to be attractive with that beautiful song!

Chapter Four

The [Apache] Indians always waited until after the summer rains to go on the warpath, when there was plenty of feed for their horses and *mescal*[4] for themselves. [In 1882] the rains had been abundant, and conditions were ideal for a raid.

One evening after Alice had gone to bed, Tom sat reading to her. The baby, who had been fretful all day, lay quietly sleeping in her crib in the corner. Suddenly [there was] a loud knock on the door, and Dutchie opened it, saying, "A runner has just come in from Globe with word that the Indians are out again and headed this way. Are you going to take your family to the tunnel where the other women and children have gone, or do you want to take them to town? The buckboard is waiting."

"To the tunnel," Alice answered, jumping out of bed. She ran to the baby, who had awakened and began to cry. She dressed hurriedly and, holding the baby close to her, followed Tom, who, with the help of Dutchie, carried bedding and clothing to the tunnel that ran south. A branch tunnel turned sharply east, and it was in this branch tunnel the women and children had gathered.

Over the entrance a blanket had been hung, so that if the Indians did come, they couldn't see the light from the one candle that served best to make "darkness visible."

West had refused to let the men move him to a place of

---

4 An intoxicating, hallucinatory drink prepared by the distillation of the fermented juices of the American aloe or maguey plants.

safety, nor would he let his wife and children go with them to the tunnel. He told them, "If the Indians come, you are to come here, where you will get the guns. That will be time enough to move me then."

"Come here!" [scoffed] one of the men as they left West's house. "Watch *me* stay right in a safe tunnel."

Tom placed the mattress on the ground near the [tunnel] opening, with the head closest to the canvas, for which Alice was thankful. The air was better there. She lay down, hugging and comforting the baby.

In the corner diagonally across from the one in which she was lying, the candle had been placed on the ground. Alice had lain there for some time, listening intently, [when] suddenly she saw spiders, bugs, and crickets, all white from being underground. They were crawling slowly along the ceiling and side walls, and [they were] all were coming in her direction! The place had been abandoned for some time, and the light had evidently disturbed them. Because her corner was the darkest they were all headed that way.

[The insects] seemed very weak. One would crawl for a little way, then rest, and another would start. One spider, that in his more prosperous days must have been a big fellow, came along the ceiling over Alice's bed. He would lose his hold with one or two of his feet, hang by the others and rest, then draw himself up again and take another step. There were not many [insects], and it would have been a small matter to kill them, but Alice seemed only half-conscious of them in her greater anxiety about the Indians.

Back from the entrance to the main tunnel, the men stood on guard with rifles ready. The mothers heard every sound throughout the long night, while the children slept peacefully and were ready for action next morning. Two nights were spent [in the tunnel] before a runner came to tell them that the Indians had passed on the [McMillan] side of the mountain and the danger was past.

Mrs. West told Alice that she and her father had walked from one window to another, watching, all through those two awful nights. They had planned that, at the first sign of Indians, they would take the children, run to the tunnel, and leave West to his fate.

❧

"Guess we'll have to wait for our payday this month," Tom said one day as he sat down to dinner. "The mail carrier just came in with word that Andy Hall was shot this morning and the express box stolen."

"Who is Andy Hall?" asked Alice.

"The express messenger whom everyone liked. When his murderers are found I'm afraid it will go hard with them, and it should. We will get all the news when the paper comes."

[*Ed. Alice wrote, by way of explanation*:] Globe lies north of the highest point of the Pinals. In 1882, before this murder was committed, George Scott had sold the Pioneer Mine on the southern slope of the mountain to a [Howard Mining] company that built a road connecting with the Dripping Springs Valley road.

A toll road was built from Globe to Pioneer, which cut off that night ride from the journey. While this road was in the course of construction, the mail and express had been brought over this shorter route on pack animals under the care of Andy Hall.

When the [newspaper] arrived, it gave a full account of the tragedy. [*Ed. The killers of Hall, two Grimes brothers and a man named Hawley, were arrested by a posse and stood trial in Globe. Hawley and young Grimes were hanged from a tree that grew in the middle of Globe's Main Street. Some of the law-abiding citizens brought the elder Grimes' wife and five little hair-lipped boys and pleaded with the mob to let the law take its course. He was turned over to the sheriff to stand trial.*]

Perhaps the sight of those five little hair-lipped boys had turned the tables in favor of their father, for what would Globe do with five little hair-lipped boys? Who would have them?

The elder Grimes was judged insane and sent to Stockton, California, as Arizona had no asylum at that time. He escaped, and was never, to Alice's knowledge, found.

When West was about again, although still on crutches, he came to the shop. After glaring about for a moment, he said, "Now, get to work. Too damned much loafing around here when I'm away."

Tom, who had just begun his day's work, stopped, laid down his hammer, took off his apron, and said, "I'm glad that I don't have to work for your kind, West."

Picking up his belongings, Tom left the shop. He helped Alice pack. Even the canvas was torn from the house, and everything was made ready to leave on the afternoon buckboard.

It was a tiresome ride. A few miles out of Globe, the driver stopped in a wide place on the road to let a team pass. A man in a buggy, driving a handsome span of horses, also stopped and twisted the lines about his hand. Throwing his leg over the end of the seat, he asked, "How's everything in the Basin?"

"Cold," replied the driver.

"Well, have a little something to warm you up." He produced a bottle. "Give the lady some first," he ordered, as the driver started to take a drink.

Alice refused the refreshments. As the bottle was returned, the man said, "Do you know that you are looking at Bill Anderson, your next County Treasurer? And this," pointing to a man beside him, "is Hen Henderson, running

for justice of the peace. He was justice of the peace in Texas."
Turning to his companion, he asked, "How long was you justice of the peace to home, Hen?"

"Ten years," the man answered. Alice judged
Henderson to be about twenty-five, and wondered how
young they allowed judges to occupy the bench in Texas.

"Well, I must be getting along, got a lot of ballots to leave
down here to a farm house. So long. See you tomorrow,
Election Day. Vote for me for County Treasurer."

"He packs good liquor," said the driver as they continued on their way.

The sky was overcast with clouds, and the wind blew
the dust into their faces as they rode up Globe's one rough,
narrow street. The west side of this street was occupied by
saloons, which were of uniform build: one story, with square,
false fronts, which extended three or four feet above the
ridgepole of the building, to give it apparent greater height.

The street in front of these saloons was full of men who
gestured wildly and talked in loud tones as they passed in
and out of the saloons.

The Curnows stopped at the Pascoe Hotel. The stairs
that passed from the front door straight up to the second
story were so narrow that but one person could comfortably
pass at a time. Their footsteps echoed on the bare floor of the
empty hall. A bracket lamp at the head of the stairs gave just
enough light to permit them to find the door of their room in
the front of the hotel.

It was very gloomy late that November day, as it had
begun to rain just as they arrived.

Tom went out to get a paper. Returning, he said, "[J.H.]
Pascoe wants me to work for him tomorrow, for sheriff. He
will pay me ten dollars to drive a team to get the voters out. I
can do nothing about building our house, since there is so
much excitement over this election. One fellow, Fred Hatch,

has bet a very good house and lot that Pascoe will be defeated. Then, too, the prospects are for rain."

"I hope it won't rain," Alice said. "This room is dreary enough without that. If the cracks in the floor got much wider, the baby may fall through. And those dark walls! Why, do you suppose, did they select dark brown paper when that little window won't give enough light to read by, even if it wasn't raining?"

"Now, don't be cross. I'll get you out of here just as soon as I can after tomorrow. But the lumberman told me that he wouldn't be open tomorrow. Too much excitement."

"I know you will get me out of here as soon as you can, Tom, but living in a hotel at four dollars a day, I feel that I should have a window with a curtain that I could roll up. I suppose that's because I've been without a window for so long, but this one has a cord over that groove in the end of the roller, then over this button-like contrivance, fastened on the window frame that has stretched so that they have tied a knot in it, which prevents the curtain from being rolled to the top or pulled down to the bottom.

"Oh, I guess I am cross, but if it rains tomorrow I will be lonesome with you away all day."

The prediction for rain on Election Day proved correct. All day long there was a steady downpour. This did not, however, dampen the election excitement. Groups of men stood in the rain and gestured and argued outside the voting place, which was opposite the hotel. Tom stopped only long enough to eat lunch, and by night his clothes were thoroughly soaked.

"I tried to collect," he told Alice, "but Pascoe wants to wait to see how the election goes, meaning, I suppose, that if he loses he will not pay at all. Well, I've surely earned the money."

The excitement did not die with the election, but was continued [the] next day in every saloon in town. In one, where the deed for the house and lot and the money of the owner's opponent were held, feeling ran high. The house owner [Hatch], contending that since Pascoe received 495 votes and the man who ran against him got 455, and there were but 436 votes in the county, refused to pay.

No one had any use for a gambler who tried to "crawfish" out of a bet. Even his friends said, "It's your own fault. Why didn't you have your friends vote oftener? That's where you lost out, and it serves you right. It's your own fault. You didn't tend to business."

This but added to the trouble. Both men, who before the election had been firm friends, left the saloon vowing vengeance on each other. They soon returned, well armed, and began shooting, until Hatch fell mortally wounded and Sam Bullock gave himself up.

When the jury was being selected, the judge called to one of the jurymen, "You go home and put on your coat."

Someone else was put in his place, and the trial proceeded. After the jury had retired to decide on a verdict, they could be heard in the courtroom, loudly arguing [about] something. Afterward one of them explained, "It was a technical point. We all knew that Sam wasn't guilty."

[The jury] called the bailiff to ask for instructions from the judge, who wrote something on a paper and sent it to the jury. Silence followed its reception, only a murmur [was heard] once in a while. Finally the bailiff brought the message back to the judge, saying, "They want you to tell them what this says. They can't none of them read it."

The judge adjusted his glasses, and indignantly took the message. He studied it for a few moments, and then, calmly laying it aside, he said, "I can't either, now, it's too cold."

The verdict was justifiable homicide. The prisoner was acquitted. Those old settlers were loath to sacrifice unnecessarily any of the scanty population.

It was four days later, when another trial was in progress, that the juryman who had been sent home for his coat appeared with it hanging over his arm. The judge thundered, "You are fined for contempt of court!"

"Who? Me? What for?"

"I told you four days ago to go home and put on your coat."

"Well, here's the coat. Here it is."

"Where do you live?"

"Up in Payson. Takes two days to go and two days to come."

"Case dismissed," said the judge.

While Tom was building the house [in Globe], life in that hotel was worse than it had been in Richmond Basin, much more dreary. To sit in that dark room all day was depressing to Alice. There was dark brown oilcloth on the top of the large dry goods box that served as a washstand, with its sides proclaiming, "E.F. Kellner, Globe, Arizona."

E. F. KELLNER.
GLOBE, A. T.
JOBBER IN GENERAL MERCHANDISE.

E. F. KELLNER & CO.	E. F. KELLNER & CO.
McMillen, A. T.	*Richmond, A. T.*
General Merchants	General Merchants
—AND—	—AND—
MINERS' OUTFITS.	MINERS' OUTFITS.

E. F. KELLNER,	E. F. KELLNER,
PROPRIETOR	*Globe, A. T.*
PINAL CREEK SAW MILLS,	LUMBER YARD.
Pinal Mountains, A. T.	Mining Timber, Lumber, Shingles, Etc.

CORRESPONDENTS:	
H. K. & F. B. THURBER & Co., New York.	WELLS, FARGO & Co's BANK, San Francisco.

E.F. Kellner advertisement. *McKenney's Pacific Coast directory 1886-1887.*

Even the stove had taken on a coat of a brown shade. It was about two feet long, with [a] flat top and bottom and bulging sides. [A] door in the end opened over a hearth so small that the ashes had fallen on the floor, and [they] showed the track of the broom, which had not very successfully removed them. [The stove] legs were placed on bricks to prevent fire in the floor, and for the same reason it was set four feet from the wall, its pipe going straight up through the ceiling.

Alice didn't know why, but the straight-backed chair was not painted brown; [however], having to sit on it, she could not enjoy its cheerful natural color.

Tom came in. She called to him, "Come here. If I look in this corner [of the mirror], I have a long, long nose and chin, with very small eyes on the top of my head. In this other corner, my nose is pug; I have no chin, but nice large eyes, if they were not crossed. Now, why that mirror?"

Tom looked at his own reflection and laughed. He was happy, telling Alice how much he had accomplished. "The material is all on the ground now, and the foundation is laid. You will have one near neighbor, a Mrs. George Scholefield. I met George today, he seems to be a nice follow."

Tom washed and tidied up a bit, then carried the baby down to the dining room. After dinner, Alice said, "Tomorrow I'm going to bundle up the baby and go with you. If I get tired I can come back by myself."

"But it's too cold for the baby. You would both freeze down there. The wind blows from the mountain, and after that rain it's colder than ever. [Besides], it's about a half-mile from town. You'd better wait until I get the house finished."

"I can help with the house. I can hand you nails and hold boards. Will you have any posts to set? You know I'm a good post-setter."

"No, I think not. I'll tell you, I'll make a tent house for

you of that canvas we bought with us, and set up the cook stove. Do you suppose you can keep warm in a tent?"

"I can't keep warm here. Although I'm putting wood in the stove all the time, I can't get the room warm."

"[Because] it's so high and has a cloth ceiling."

"How high is it?"

"The room is about twelve feet square, perpendicularly as well as horizontally. Makes it look like a box, doesn't it? Well, I will quit working on the house and build a tent house for you tomorrow."

"We can move in the next day, can we? And I will meet my neighbor down there."

"Perhaps so, if I get the tent finished."

The next night tent house was ready. Tom said, "I'm sorry, dear, but that Mrs. Scholefield is crazy as a bat. While I was waiting for the posts for the tent [to set], I walked down to the Scholefield place, where I saw some chickens in the yard. You know my weakness for chickens, so I knocked on the door. She opened it and I asked, 'Will you sell me a few of your chickens?'

"She looked up at the doorframe above her head and answered, 'I don't know where it is.'

"I was astonished. Again I asked if she would sell any chickens, and again she stared up at the doorframe saying, 'Guess he's got it with him,' and [she] shut the door in my face.

"I stood there looking at her without saying a word when [again] she said, 'Guess he's got it in his pocket,' and shut the door in my face."

"Oh, isn't that dreadful! Is there was no other woman in the neighborhood?"

"I don't know. But you can keep away from her."

"Why, I would just as soon be among the Indians as with a crazy woman." But Alice was glad to move into the tent house the next day, [from where] she watched the progress of the house building.

Alice cooked supper in the tent house and was just preparing the baby for bed when Tom came in, followed by Mr. and Mrs. Scholefield. After introducing them to his wife, Tom said, """George and I are going up town. I must get locks for the doors. The man who is helping me will put them in tomorrow. Mrs. Scholefield will stay with you," and he went into the partly finished house to change his clothes.

Alice was terrified to be left with this crazy woman! What was Tom thinking of? She managed to answer George's questions, and Mrs. Scholefield joined intelligently in the conversation. This, Alice thought, is one of her lucid moments. George was saying something about planting trees, and how he had his chicken yards built. [Mrs. Scholefield] would say something about the eggs they got, but Alice was thinking of that crazy woman.

George said, "There is going to be a dance Friday night at the schoolhouse. You and Tom better come along with us. We always have a good time."

Alice hesitated. "How could I? What would I do with the baby?"

Mrs. Scholefield suddenly said, "You'll have to keep the chickens out of there, because I'm going to plant flowers on the side."

Alice was panic-stricken again. George turned to his wife and said in a very loud voice, "Oh, Clit, we're not talking about that now. I was telling Mrs. Curnow about the dance we are going to this week."

Then, turning to Alice, "She's as deaf as a bat. Guess your husband thought she was crazy yesterday when he was talking about chickens, and she thought he was the man from the smelter asking for the key to the blacksmith shop at the mill that I am watching.

"They have no blacksmith shop at the smelter, and I let them use ours. The key always hangs on the doorframe, and

that was what she was looking for. We had a good laugh
when Tom explained to her tonight."

Alice was greatly relieved! It turned out to be a pleasure,
for [she and Mrs. Scholefield] became great friends.

They did go to that dance. The movable partition was
taken out, and the seats and desks were unfastened and
placed in the back of the room, where the babies slept peacefully while their mothers enjoyed themselves. One at a time,
their fathers tiptoed back to see that all was well with them.

[*Ed. According to Gila County records, Curnow and
Scholefield purchased a lot and a frame building in Globe that was
being used as a saloon in April 1886. Mrs. Curnow did not mention
this transaction or any businesses in which they may have been
associated.*]

⚜

There was a heavy fall of snow on the Pinal Mountains
every winter. Water ran in Pinal Creek that runs through
[Globe] until late in August, when it was dry for about three
weeks. The summer rains again brought a stream of water
through the town.

Only those who lived there at that time could appreci-
ate what the forest fires, the sawmills, and the herds of cattle
accomplished in their destruction of a beautiful country. [At
first] the growth of grass was so heavy that the [Indian
women] cut it with hoes and brought bundles of it on their
backs, to sell in town.

Alice remembered well the first time she saw a sheet of
water coming over the hill in front of their home. She
thought there had been a cloudburst, but after that every
shower came down the hill in the same way. Years later, in a
bulletin from the Arizona University, she read an explanation
of the phenomenon: The range had been overstocked and
the cattle had eaten the grass down to the roots, leaving nothing to stop the rain from running off the land. [It took] the

seeds that might have restored the growth. Then, Arizona's hills were bare.

The bank that was started in Globe by Southerland and Fish had not prospered. It failed, not for lack of customers, but [because] people preferred [to invest in] cattle. Nearly everyone owned a few. Buying a few at a time, Tom Curnow had acquired quite a herd. He decided to move on a ranch near the [San Pedro] River. Alice was to remain in Globe until the house was ready, where [Murray, their second child,] was born on November 4, 1884.

It was February before the house was ready and [Alice moved]. The high back seat of the buckboard had no springs and was very uncomfortable. On this she rode, holding her baby (Murray) in her arms, and her little daughter (Alice) on the seat beside her. [Little Alice] needed as much attention as the baby, as there was nothing around the floor of the buckboard to keep her from falling out if she should slip down.

The road ran up a very steep part of the Pinal Mountains, and the driver stopped frequently to rest his animals. Regardless of what Tom had said about it, Alice had expected to see tall pine trees near the top of the mountain. But there was nothing but a forest of tall stumps. Some had been burned and their stark, blackened, and mutilated bodies completed a scene of desolation.

The trip up the mountains, with frequent stops, had not only rested the horses, but Alice, too. Going down the other side there were no restful stops and they traveled all the time. To keep little Alice from falling out [was] an exhausting task, and the journey [took] all day.

Alice was so glad when her husband met the stage. He was driving a farm wagon, and the seat had springs! Tom held little Alice on his knee while he told Alice what a proficient cook he had become. "I have bacon and beans cooked, and all I have to do when we get home is to make bread. You should see me! I don't bother cutting out biscuits, I just put the dough in the bake pan and smooth it out."

Alice accepted his offer to prepare the meal while she lay on a couch in the kitchen and watched him, too tired to move another step. Tom demonstrated his method of making bread. When he had smoothed it in the pan, he rubbed flour over his hands, letting the little rolls drop [onto] the mixture, where they baked very hard. When it was baked, he took it out of the oven and wrapped it up in a very dirty hand towel, but even that didn't arouse Alice to protest. She was just tired.

After helping Alice with the children, Tom sat beside her bed, smoking his pipe and telling her how much he had accomplished. "Wait till morning and see the great field of grain, coming up fine and all fenced. Three of the cattlemen have gone in with me in the grain, and we are going to take out a ditch to bring water from the [San Pedro]. We'll have to irrigate if it doesn't rain, and we can't risk it. And this house. I built that, too.

"Of course we will have a real one just as soon as I have time to go to Tucson for the lumber. The grain had to be in or we wouldn't have a crop this year."

That night Alice took no interest, even in the house, for which Tom was apologizing. He smoked in pleased silence for a few moments, then added, "I forgot to mention the well at the back door and a stockade corral I have ready."

[The] next morning, in looking things over, Alice quite agreed with her husband that it was more important to get the grain in first. What a lovely field it was, stretching from in front of the house down toward the river. On the left was a forest of old mesquite trees that reminded her of an aged apple orchard in Maine.

Behind the house the rolling hills were covered with desert growth, with the tall saguaro [cactus] towering above them all. It had been a good year, with plenty of rain and snow in the mountains, and everything looked green and thriving. Alice was not going to be lonesome here!

She turned to the house, which was not so pleasing to look at. There was a good floor and [it had] big windows. The two rooms were sixteen feet long, a fine start for that home that they were going to build, but just then the walls were bare and there was no ceiling under the roof. Not having enough lumber, the partition extended but part way across between the rooms, but the carpet marked the outline of the bedroom. The house was pleasantly situated. Having much to do, Alice was content—or rather, she had no time to be discontented.

High mountains surrounded the valley where the Curnows lived. In February the thermometer would register ninety during the day, and [then it would] freeze at night. As the season advanced, this great difference in temperature disappeared. It was hot at night, too, and *much* hotter during the day.

There was no rain during March, but a sprinkle in April, and in spots the grain began to look yellow. Tom and his partners worked desperately, putting in the ditch. They had started at the field and were about two miles from the house.

One night on their way home their neighbors stopped, and Mr. [William] Steffy said, "Mrs. Curnow, there is a band of Indians on their way to gather the fruit from the saguaro. Pay no attention to them and they will not molest you. None but friendly Indians come in this direction."

The next day the Indians arrived, some on horseback and some on foot, all carrying long poles with which to get the fruit that grows on the very top of the tall saguaro. The [women] also carried babies on their backs and walked, while the [men] rode their ponies.

Alice was hanging out her washing and didn't notice [the Indians] until they were beside her. According to [the] instructions from Mr. Steffy, she pretended not to see them.

She picked up her pan, went into the house, and—she supposed to impress them with her indifference to their presence—she left the door open.

This must have surprised and encouraged them, for four of the [women] followed Alice. Pressing their faces against the window, they looked in. Alice, pretending bravery which she didn't feel, still ignored them.

They boldly entered the house and, closing the door, they sat on the floor with their backs to it. In their harsh, cackle-like voices [they] were evidently discussing Alice's housekeeping, which was giving them much amusement. Alice was trembling so she could scarcely stand.

One of [the women] shuffled to her feet, which was done by first getting on all fours, and started toward the bed. Little Alice screamed and clutched her mother's skirt. Her fear must have aroused Alice's protective instinct, for, picking up her water bucket, she started toward them, saying "You-ca-shee," [Phonetic] meaning in Indian, "Go away."

Alice didn't know if this word was spelled correctly, but it had the desired effect. [The four women] scrambled to their feet and left at once, calling derisively at her as they went. After that she always shouted "You-ca-shee" as soon as an Indian approached her house, and they always obeyed.

Chapter Five

Their market was twelve miles up the river and on the other side, where one store, which was also the post office, was called Dudleyville. Alice took the children and went with Tom in the farm wagon, the only one they had, to do some shopping.

Tom went into the store to inquire where they could get something to eat, and while he was gone a pleasant-looking, dark-complexioned young man got in the wagon beside Alice. [He said] "I'm Jack Brannaman. I'm going to take you over to the house to get something to eat. Tom, he'll come along with Bob."

As he turned the team to leave the yard, he called Mrs. Curnow's attention to an old Indian man, who was driving into the place in a farm wagon full of women and children. A red handkerchief was tied around his head to keep his long hair back.

"That's old Eskiminzin," her companion informed her. "He's a neighbor of yours, across the river from you. He's a civilized old brute of an Indian. Them're his wives and children riding with him.

"Here's how we know he's civilized: He used to visit a white man [Charles McKinney] down the river here. One day he went to see the white man, who was just sitting down to dinner. [The white man] asked old Eskiminzin to eat with him. After his meal the Indian went outside and turned round and shot the white man dead.

"At his trial he said, 'I shoot this man because I love him and my heart swell. Anyone can shoot his enemy, but it takes

Eskiminzin, Chief of the Aravaipa Apaches. *Arizona Historical Society/ Tucson, #22231, Wood Collection.*

a brave man to shoot his friend.' To the jury this must have proved that old Eskiminzin was civilized, for they found him not guilty. He has been allowed to live off the reservation ever since.

"He's scared to death when the Indians are on the warpath, and he always comes with his family here to Dudleyville for protection."

Alice never learned what Eskiminzin had done to the other Indians to cause this fear.

By this time they were riding into the home yard of George Scott, Brannaman's stepfather, who had located and then sold the Pioneer Mine. Scott owned a large ranch, with a fruit orchard and a garden full of all kinds of vegetables. The long, low adobe house with a porch in front was in the midst of a grove of tall trees that met overhead, entirely shading the house. A ditch full of water ran past the door, in which some ducks were enjoying a swim.

Mr. Scott invited the Curnows to take dinner with him, and they were glad to accept. It was noon but quite dark in the dining room. Coming in from the bright sunshine, Alice could see only that there were a number of people seated around the long table. At first she thought Mr. Scott was having a meeting of some kind, or a party, but after becoming accustomed to the dim light, she saw that they were all men, evidently laborers, who were quietly eating their dinner.

Many Indians and derelict white men found a haven on George Scott's ranch. One of these white men came in while they were at dinner, and in a rather apologetic manner mentioned, "I just got bit with a rattlesnake." He was holding up his thumb.

Scott laughed softly as, turning to Alice, he said, "That's the fourth time this week Ben Black has been bitten by a rattlesnake. I believe he keeps one [on hand] for that purpose. You see, that's the only way he can get enough whiskey. You know, I couldn't let a man die of snakebite when I have an extra quart of the stuff."

Turning to the man, he said, "All right, Black, help yourself."

Black must have helped himself plenty, for he was sleeping audibly when they passed him lying under a tree about an hour later.

When the Curnows left for home they found their wagon loaded with fruit and vegetables from the Scott ranch. This was a great treat, as they had nothing growing.

No rain! May came in so hot that each morning Alice dreaded to see the sun come up. It was copper-colored. It came up over the hill like a burst of flame, searing and burning everything up. The Curnows watched the sky every day, hoping for a sign of rain, but there wasn't a cloud to be seen.

Their neighbor's cattle that had been roaming all over the valley had gone to the hills for food. It was so far to the river for water that they soon began to show signs of weakness as they followed the trail down from the hills. Each day they had to go farther and farther to find food. Sometimes they were too weak to get back to water, and died on the way.

Alice's little son, Murray, was dressed only in a diaper. He passed the heat of the day slapping a clean rag in a pan of clean water on the floor beside him. It was too hot to let little Alice outside to play, although she pleaded to go, and [she] always accompanied her mother when she went for water. From the number of rattlesnakes Tom had killed, Alice thought it not quite safe [outside], so she put up a swing in the opening where the partition in the house was to be.

This was little Alice's only amusement, except when Alice would read to her from *Sunshine*, a prize book from a San Francisco store. Her favorite story was "The Three Little Pigs," quite as interesting in 1885, Alice thought, as it had become in 1934 [when she was writing].

Alice was alone with the children all day. Tom and their neighbors left early in the morning and worked as long as they could see, desperately trying to get the ditch finished in time to save the grain, on which yellow spots were spreading wider every day. And still there was no rain. The river was getting low.

At last the emergency grew so great that the men abandoned the plan of digging the ditch farther up the river to the water level, and [they] built a dam to turn the water in on the land. They built cribs of cottonwood trees that grew along the bank of the river. After these were placed and filled with rock and dirt, the dam was wide enough to drive a team across.

It was successful. The water came down on the great field, but it was too late to save the crop. The horses were turned in on the grain, as the range feed had dried up.

The men worked bravely on for the next harvest, which was to be corn.

⁂

One day while the men were planting, Alice heard the buzz of a rattlesnake. Out in their front yard one was coiled, as their cat stood with its back humped, watching it. This was the first live rattlesnake Alice had seen, and she was sure that anyone who has ever heard that sound would realize how terrifying it was.

She screamed and screamed, until the men came running from the field and killed [the snake]. Later, she thought it was fortunate that this happened, as it terrified her daughter [and she learned a lesson] to see her mother so frightened.

Later in the summer, Alice was hanging out her washing. Little Alice, as usual, had accompanied her. She was digging under a tree nearby when Alice heard a rattler and the little girl scream at the same time. She ran to the child, asking, "Did it bite you?"

As Alice caught her daughter to her, [she answered] through her tears, "No, but it said it would."

The snake was just crawling over a log. Alice hated to let it get away, so [she] threw a rock at it. [The snake] instantly dropped back into a coil, but rattled no more. Little Alice rang the cowbell, which was the signal for her father that they needed him.

While Alice waited for Tom she experimented with that rattlesnake. It ran its tongue out over its body as it watched her as closely as she was watching it, while at a safe distance from the creature. She discovered that while her body was perfectly still, its tongue would run in and out of its mouth, but if she moved the least bit, ever so slowly, without moving her feet, the snake would stop moving its tongue. When she moved back in the same slow movement, the tongue would perform again.

Tom came running. After killing [the snake], he cut off its head. With two sticks Alice pried [the snake's] mouth open and found the fangs turned back against the roof of its mouth.

She examined the place where Little Alice had been digging. It was not more than two feet from the depression in the sand where the snake had been coiled. She still trembled when she thought about it, years later.

With all the crawlers that inhabit the Arizona desert, none of

Alice's children were ever bitten or stung by any of them.

At first, Tom cut the rattles from every rattlesnake he killed. The Curnows tied them together and hung them on a picture frame, until they became too numerous to bother with. But they left those hanging on the picture frame.

One night Alice heard the rattle of a snake in the room with them. Tom was a heavy sleeper, and she had difficulty in waking him. When she told him [about the sound], he threw the covers back, and she had to hold him while she explained that the snake was in the house. He was going to jump out of bed.

"Wait," Alice said, "it might be right beside the bed. Light the lamp and let us watch."

The lamp was on a stand beside the bed, and Tom lighted it. Not a sound, but they waited. Presently they heard the rattle again, [and] she saw a little mouse on the picture frame, gnawing the rattles. After that they threw the rattles away. Rattlesnakes had ceased to be a curiosity to them.

❦

The men worked hard for the next crop, and hope came again to those toilers. They were not the only toilers! Alice seemed to be always washing. It was so hot that a frequent change of clothes was necessary, and the water had to be pulled out of the well in a bucket. Between that and cooking and caring for her babies, Alice was a very busy woman. Oh, but the home they were going to have!

Planning was such a comfort, even if its realization never came to pass.

They had watched the grain come up and wither, and now they watched the corn. One evening Tom said, "I shall have to go to Globe and sell more of the cattle. We need more money."

My, [Alice thought] what a lot of money that ranch had swallowed up, and with no pleasure in the spending.

"Steffy will to sleep up here for your protection. He sleeps outside anyhow, so it will not inconvenience him any. He offered to come. So you and the children will be safe."

When Tom returned from Globe, he had sold all the cattle. Alice was bathing [Murray] when he rode up to the door saying, "Here's the check for the cattle. Take care of it, will you? I paid all the bills. Don't owe a cent to anyone."

Then, as he turned his horse from the door, he added, "Steffy wants me in a hurry. I'll be right back and tell you all the news from Globe."

Holding her wet baby in her arms, Alice put the check, all the money they had in the world, behind the cups in the corner cupboard. She forgot all about it until several days later when Tom was going to Dudleyville. Then they both hunted, but no check could be found. They were desperately anxious!

Alice took everything out of her trunk numberless times, for she could think of no other place that she would [have] put it. Tom feared that she had burned it with trash. She was again emptying everything out of her trunk, and opening every old letter when Tom, who had made some coffee, noticed the check behind the cups. The shelf was too high for her to see on top of it without a chair! That was one reason, Alice supposed, that she had put it there.

The corn [crop] was a success, and that fall the men again planted grain. "No danger of failure this time," said Tom, "There's plenty of water from the [river]."

He was always an early riser, and one morning when everything was going fine, he had gone down to the corral. Alice didn't know where he was, as often he would walk up the ditch to see that it was clear of obstructions.

She had just attended to her baby and she was laying him on the pillow when she heard a soft step at her back door. Looking through one of the cracks that had developed in that partial partition, behind which the bed was placed, she saw a young Indian man with nothing on but a g-string, (as the usually very dirty rag passed between the legs, then through a string around the waist, was called), coming in her back door.

She shouted "You-ca-shee," but with a smile that showed his white teeth, he came quickly on. Alice had kept step with him along the bed, until he got to the end of the partition, where he had to go around her dining table. By that time she realized that he had no regard for "You-ca-shee."

Alice had never been athletic, but she jumped over the foot of her bed, ran across that open space in her nightgown, and grabbed the loaded pistol, which for her protection was always placed on the shelf under which their clothes were hung.

She pointed it straight at him, saying, "Now, you You-ca-shee."

He needed no second bidding. He backed quickly to the door, from which he turned and ran so fast that his long black hair and his g-string stood straight out behind him!

Tom said the Indian must have been watching the house, as he knew just where to find him in the corral. In sign language, [the Indian] made Tom understand what Alice had done. Tom told him that she was *loco*, meaning in Spanish that she was crazy.

After that, no Indian ever came near the house. They think that a crazy person is bewitched or possessed of the devil and can harm them. If they had occasion to go down the valley, they went on the other side of the river.

❧

Christmas that year found the Curnows with very little cash, with none to spare for celebrations. As one old farmer expressed it, "A Tucson banker had his hand on their crop," meaning a mortgage.

Alice had put the children in bed and sat down to play crib with Tom, all the time wondering how they could make a Christmas for little Alice.

"How about Christmas, Tom?"

"I've been wondering about that, too. We can't buy much, but how would a rustic chair and table do, with a chair for her doll?"

"Her doll is broken."

"Well, can't you make a rag doll? She would like it just as well, I suppose. Would you like to see the legs I have ready for the chair? They are out in the corncrib."

Tom lighted the lantern and they went out to see the lovely legs that he had found in limbs of mesquite trees. They matched beautifully. "These are for the chair, he said, "They curve just right for the back. I shall sandpaper the bark off them."

That night after Tom had gone to sleep, Alice lay there making and dressing that rag doll [in her mind], when suddenly she remembered a [cash] balance she had, then more than a year old, in a store in New York.

She got out of bed to look for it and, sure enough, there was nineteen cents due her! Fine. She would have to make a body, as she found a head in their catalogue for that price.

And what a Christmas little Alice had! Alice doubted if she ever enjoyed one more. The stocking, which she had hung on the foot of her crib, was filled with homemade candy, and fruits. The table, her chair, and the doll in the chair waiting for breakfast to be served filled her heart with joy.

✾

Things drifted along happily after that. The grain was doing fine, the chickens were laying, and the family had plenty to eat. The Curnows were quite happy with the outlook.

One morning in February, as Alice set the coffee pot on the table and looked out of the window toward the river, which on their side could not be seen until it passed around the bend of their field. The bank was high and steep there. Alice saw the water, level with their field. Logs and trees were tumbling along.

"Look!" she exclaimed, pointing toward the river. Tom jumped up from the table and looked out the window.

"Are those logs?" she asked him, for she could hardly believe her eyes.

Tom replied, "Yes. And I believe they are from our dam. After breakfast I'll hitch up the team and go see."

"And I'll go with you."

There was no more conversation. Alice believed she had ceased thinking. She wanted to see [what had happened]. Tom was silent as they rode in the farm wagon to the dam.

The [San Pedro] River had taken a new course, leaving their dam high and dry. In later years Alice was reminded of that moment, when she saw the fine bridge near Florence left out on the desert when the Gila [River] went meandering over the country, finding a new route to the sea.

The Curnows sat there, looking at the wreck of their hopes. Tom got out of the wagon and walked along the dam, which, firm and strong, had withstood the flood. Even the foundation was high above the river. He got down to examine it, saying something to Alice, but she couldn't hear him over the roar of the water.

Tom came back, got into the wagon, and drove away from the river. "The dam stood, all right," he said. "We did a good job, but that river in flood is like bucking the ocean. Well, we must begin all over again. Too bad, after all our hard work."

Alice asked, "Where do we begin?"

"Back in Globe, I suppose."

"Let us go today," Alice suggested.

"I think it will take all day to get ready, but we will try to leave early in the morning."

When calamities had come upon her, Alice seemed stunned. She could form no opinion or make new plans. By the time her faculties returned, things were righting themselves. But this she did know: That she wanted to get away from them at once, turn her back upon them and never look back.

Tom and Alice spent the day preparing for their journey. Her only interest was in packing her trunk and preparing a lunch, for in a farm wagon it would take two days to make the trip to Globe.

Tom turned the chickens over to the care of Tom Desmond, their neighbor. Alice might have said that he gave them to Desmond and never received a penny for them. When the grain was ripe, Desmond refused to let the man to whom they had sold it into the field to cut it, [causing] trouble. So the Curnows lost everything they had on the ranch.

Even the grocery man in Dudleyville, George Cook, tried to cheat them. Alice wrote to him at once, telling him about their moving to Globe and acknowledging a bill of fifty dollars, which they would pay at the rate of ten dollars a month. Cook acknowledged the first two payments. On the third he sent a receipt saying, "Said to have paid ten dollars," after Alice had written about it.

As the postmaster in Globe had seen her enclose the money, and Cook was the next postmaster to receive it, Alice wrote that she would have to take it up with the postal authorities, as one of the postmasters must be robbing the mail. This had the desired effect: Mr. Cook sent the receipt for ten dollars.

It was a hard pull up the mountains, and Mr. Steffy

Sultan Bros. Store, Globe, Arizona. *Arizona Historical Society/Tucson, #62526.*

offered the loan of another span of horses if the Curnows would take a case of his eggs to sell in Globe. Tom accepted Steffy's offer. The extra horses would make the trip much easier. Tom left Alice at her sister's home in Globe while he went to town to dispose of the eggs.

While living in Globe they had done their shopping with David Sultan, who had sent his bill to them and which Tom had paid at the time he sold the cattle. Tom didn't have the bill with him, but knowing Dave Sultan, he had [not] asked for a receipt when he met him and paid Dave on the street. But Sultan had dropped dead during the Curnows' absence, so it was to Sultan's store that Tom took the eggs.

"Yes, bring them in," said Sultan Brothers, who had inherited Dave's business. After Tom delivered the eggs, the Sultan Brothers presented that old bill. He had to pay Steffy

for that case of eggs [out of his own pocket] when they needed the money so badly.

Alice didn't pack anything before leaving the ranch.
Neither of them could get away quickly enough, nor did they
ever look back. Tom sent a man down after their furniture,
and to take Steffy's horses back, while he again found work
in the Old Dominion Mine.

It was three days before their furniture came. Late that
night, after they had gotten settled in the house of two
rooms, the man's son who had accompanied him to the ranch
came to the door. In a very confidential manner he gave Alice
a large package, saying almost in a whisper, "Father forgot
this."

The package was tied with strong string. After taking off
one paper wrapping after another, Alice came to a strip of
house lining, yards and yards long. At the end of that, out
rolled Tom's teeth that had never fitted him! Alice believed
that he would have been glad to lose [them]. She was terribly
disappointed; she thought she had something precious.

The Curnows lived in two rooms, as did most of the
people in Globe at that time who were in rented houses, and
Tom went down in the mine to work.

Through mismanagement the Old Dominion did not
pay. An old man named [Alex] Trippel, an educated man but
with no business, was the manager. Several young men held
sinecure positions.

Another unnecessary expense was what Trippel called a
"blow-out," when the smelter was closed once a month and a
celebration was held, although no one knew exactly what
was being celebrated. It was very expensive to start the
smelter again, and it was a disadvantage to close it from a
business stand[point]. Every man was asked to donate a day's
pay for this celebration, when beef, bread, and an abundance
of beer were provided for anyone who wished to attend.

After the "blow-out" was over, the beer that was left (and there was always plenty of it) disappeared. No one knew who took it, and as Tom and Alice never attended, although Tom had to give a day's pay, which was four dollars, they took no interest in the beer.

A.L. Walker, just out of college, was a fine, capable man whom everyone liked and respected. He was the assistant superintendent, but he was not allowed to carry out his businesslike plans, and he left the company. After Walker left, Trippel posted a notice that the mine would have to cut expenses. One-half of the men would work the first half of the month and the other half would work the last half of the month. But he continued to hold the "blow-outs."

Tom at last refused to give for the celebrations, saying he couldn't afford to. He might not have been so independent had they known that the mine would close in a short time and they would need those four dollars!

One of the mine owners had visited Globe and learned of the inefficiency of Trippel. One of his discoveries was [made] when he went among the workmen at the smelter. He would ask, "What does Ed Lyons do?"

And each man answered, "Well, when we want anything from the storeroom we must go to Ed for the key."

"H-m-m, a large salary for a man to carry a key. Must be something very valuable in there."

The owner found others drawing salaries for just such sinecure positions. He examined the storeroom, to find only ordinary supplies for the mine and smelter. With his report made out, he returned to New York. Trippel received a written dismissal [and the mine was closed]. Everyone was hoping that Walker would be put in charge of the mine, but it remained closed.

It seemed that the Curnows' hard luck had come to stay. The Old Dominion was the only mine that had been operating, and a new baby was coming to them. The doctor's price was fifty dollars. Mrs. Sultan told Alice that a Mrs. Robertson, whom she had employed [as a midwife] when her baby was born, was just as good as a doctor. Mrs. Sultan had four children and [she] should know.

The Curnows had moved into a larger house next door to Doctor Cook, the only physician in Globe. But thinking of what that fifty dollars could do for them, Alice didn't engage him. As conditions were getting worse all the time and [the doctor] had been looking for a new location, he left town just a week before their third child, Charles, was born. Alice suffered in labor for thirty-six hours [before] someone brought another and more efficient midwife.

⁜

Little Alice and Murray had been whooping cough sufferers for several weeks before the new baby came. With faint hope of protecting the baby from [whooping cough], Mary [Alice's sister], who had married Charles Starr and was living in Globe, took the two older children home with her. Young Alice, who contracted the cough first, had recovered enough in a couple of weeks to return home, but Murray was still coughing.

[While Murray was staying with] Mary, she was giving a dinner for some friends who were leaving Globe. She took great pains in making a watermelon cake, using two of the same shape tins, one much smaller than the other and without a bottom. Into the smaller pan she poured a pink cake mixture, with raisins for seeds. Setting the smaller tin in the larger, she filled the space between with white cake mixture, and baked it.

Then, with green frosting and a wire stem covered with green paper stuck to the end of the cake, Mary had a work of art. She placed it in a stone jar with a cover and went about preparing the rest of her dinner. She heard the cover of the jar rattle and asked, "What are you doing, Murray?"

He would come to the door, and shaking his little head he would answer, "Nothing, Aunt Mary. Not anything."

And she would return to her cooking. Again the jar would rattle and the same question and answer would be given. When the time came to serve the cake the only decoration left on it was the green paper-covered wire stem!

With the mine closed, there was nothing in view but prospecting. Not [a] very encouraging [outlook], when the mines, already equipped with machinery and ore, were closing because of no market. However, many a rich mine had been discovered during one of these depressions.

Tom was preparing to leave Globe in his search for employment when he was offered assessment work in Pioneer for [W.H.] Duryea, a merchant of Globe, who would pay in groceries. They were glad [for] this chance. Tom went at once, but Alice waited until Charles was two months old.

Tom came from Pioneer to move their furniture. Alice followed the next day, again holding a new baby in her arms and holding little Alice on the high back seat of the buckboard stage. Murray, still coughing, remained with Mary in Globe.

The horses were no longer frequently changed. One span traveled all day. The Government provided sufficient means for suitable conveyance of the mail, but the contract was sublet and sublet until only the barest service could be given. Someone in the East enjoyed an unearned income, while they suffered for this graft.

The stages to and from Globe passed each other in Pioneer. That day when Alice arrived, the other two white women of the camp were waiting for the stage to take them to Globe. They begged her to return with them, as they had just been warned that the Indians were coming. Tom also pleaded with her to go back, but it had been an exhausting ride, and Alice refused to travel any farther.

Tom had to help her into the house he had provided for her, where he had dinner waiting. Alice couldn't eat; the bed was all she wanted to see. Tom waited on little Alice, and then took her outside with him, where he put up a swing for her under a lovely big tree at the end of the house.

Alice was sitting up again, ready to take her place as cook, when they came in. Little Alice was flushed and happy.

"Mother, there's the loveliest big hill right back of the house with the loveliest flowers. I'm going to pick some."

"No. You must never cross the creek," her father told her. Then, turning to Alice, he said, "Did you notice how thick the brush is there?"

"I didn't notice anything until I found this bed, but now I am ready for the sights of Pioneer. Where is this brush?"

The room she was in was eight feet square, with a very low ceiling. It was lined and papered, with one window and a door in front, against which little Alice's crib was placed, and a window in the rear. Alice's [big] bed filled up one end of the room, and the crib with a small table with a chest of drawers left very little room for company.

The kitchen had neither lining nor paper, [and] one could see the roof over it. The table, stove, washstand, and chairs filled the other rooms. [The kitchen had] no back window, but there was one in front where the door opened on the road, into which one stepped. There was no step or porch.

The Curnows went outside to look at their home from the front. It must have been built for a bunkhouse when the Pioneer Mine was running. It was six rooms long and one room wide. They had the center rooms. The back was right on the edge of the creek that was very narrow and dry, except when a sudden rain in the mountains sent a flood of water raging down, carrying everything before it. The creek was bordered with trees and shrubs, where the road ran beside it into the hills.

They were down in the bottom of a canyon, from which the hills on either side rose sharply to a great height, giving them a very short, pleasant day in summer, but it was not so good in the winter.

Chapter Six

Alice took her daughter by the hand and they walked with Tom for a short distance down the road, for a bucket of water. It came from a shed-covered shaft, over which a board was laid, which the water [level] nearly reached. Coming back they stopped in a clump of trees that grew between the house and that shed-covered shaft, where little Alice enjoyed her swing again. Pointing to the hill behind the house, Tom said, "There's the brush." The hill was covered with it, right down to the bottom of the canyon.

"Never let [little] Alice cross that creek bed. There are cats (he meant mountain lions), rattlesnakes, and there have been bears on these mountains. They might come lower down in that brush. No one has ever seen them here, but be on the safe side. Besides, she might get lost in that growth, it's tall enough."

Neither Tom nor Alice mentioned the Indians until Tom pointed to a dark hole in the hill, saying, "There is a tunnel. I swept it out this afternoon while you were resting. Do you want to sleep there tonight?"

"Do you think it necessary, Tom? You know when the Indians leave the reservation, they are always trying to get back to their old home in the mountains north of Globe, and here we are south of Globe. I don't like sleeping in tunnels. Have you seen any Indians since you've been here?"

"No, I haven't, and I have been thinking of what you say. They are always going north, but I don't like to risk you and the children being in danger."

"Let us stay in the house until we hear more about them."

Tom didn't seem to be very happy over this plan, but did-n't, Alice thought, want to appear less brave than she was. He said no more until they were preparing for bed. Then he remarked, "If we hear any disturbance, it will be at daybreak. Don't stop to dress, take the baby and I will take [little] Alice and whatever else you want, and [we will] run for that tunnel."

Alice tied up some things that the baby would need, and they went to bed. She needed no rocking, and she slept soundly until just at daybreak, [when] she was awakened by several shots. They both jumped from the bed. Alice put on her shoes, grabbed the baby, and Tom took his load. They had to run out the front door, then around the two rooms at the end of the house. Alice had just gotten to the mouth of the tunnel when they heard Mr. Sedow, a man who lived farther up the canyon, shouting to them. Tom went back to meet him.

"There are no Indians, Sedow said. "That was Black Jack Newman. He is mad because I didn't invite him into my house for protection, as I did all the rest of the men in camp. I would just as soon have an Indian in my house. He did this, had two pistols loaded and fired them just as fast as he could to frighten us. My wife (a Mexican woman) would rather have the Indians than Black Jack.

"I didn't [call] you because I knew that if they came they would attack us first and you would hear them and hide."

Tom and Alice thanked Mr. Sedow for coming to tell them. What a relief it was! They both went back to bed.

The first time Alice actually saw Black Jack, he was com-ing down the road in front of their house. He was a big, burly fellow with a mass of black, kinky hair. He wore no hat; he had heavy black eyebrows; he was clean-shaven, showing his large and ugly mouth with thick lips hanging open; and his small black eyes looked sharply about him.

Both his shirtsleeves were button-less, his shirt collar-less. His shoes, without laces, were badly run down at the heel, and he was constantly hitching up his trousers that were without suspenders or belt. Altogether, he was the most repulsive-looking person Alice had seen in a long time. She was to know more of Black Jack.

Mr. Sedow, who was a cattleman, claimed the few pigs that had been left by the boardinghouse keeper when the Pioneer Mine closed. No one else wanted them. At the time [the Curnows] moved to Pioneer, these pigs had increased to a great number and were a nuisance about the camp. Nothing could be left outside in safety. But none of the pigs had ever become so bold as to enter a house. The Curnows had no screens, nor did they need them, as the flies did not bother them much.

Mr. and Mrs. Jim Evans occupied the two rooms on the north end of their house. Mrs. Evans had but one little boy, so [she] had more time than Alice [did] to visit. She was a very small woman and always wore hoops. As she walked very fast, the hoops waved violently in and out about her. She was rather untidy about putting her groceries away. She would leave them on the kitchen floor—her bacon, flour, or any bulky things always leaned against the wall until they were used. Her home looked "womanless."

Mrs. Evans was visiting Alice one day when they heard a great commotion in her end of the house. She left hurriedly, and Alice could hear her swearing. The disturbance increased until Alice finally heard a shot. Then all was quiet. She carefully opened her door and peeked out, expecting to see a dead body. She saw Mrs. Evans coming down the road, her hoops greatly agitating as she came swinging along, with a rifle over her arm and the appearance of a conqueror.

She called to Alice, "Come down here and see what that damned hog has done to my house. I had a sack of flour sitting right here by my back door and [the hog] dragged it all over the house, even under the bed. He must have [shaken] it all the way. I'll have to take everything out. But I got that hog." And she hung up her rifle on the wall near the door.

⚜

Alice would send an order for groceries on the stage to Mr. Duryea one day, and the next day they would be delivered. One day she was sitting out under the tree where little Alice had her swing when she heard the rumble of thunder. Looking up, she could see heavy clouds on the top of the Pinals.

It didn't disturb [Alice], as it seldom rained on the south side of the mountains. Little Alice was digging in the bottom of the creek, building fences and making roads, when her mother heard a dreadful roar. She ran to the creek and instinctively took the girl's hand and led her up out of it, when she saw a great wall of water coming down.

It was quite black with the debris it had accumulated. It came in a straight wall, and Alice trembled yet when she thought of its frightfulness. She clasped little Alice to her and required [the] swing that was right behind her for support.

The stage always arrived about noon, but the day after that flood it didn't come at all. Late in the afternoon the driver came on horseback, carrying the mail and saying that the road was washed out too badly for the stage to travel. It didn't worry Alice, as she didn't want to travel, but when three days went by without any supplies coming, things began to look serious.

Mrs. Collins, her other white neighbor, came in to see her. She was very easy going, never got excited about anything. After discussing the storm, Alice asked her, "What have you got to eat, Mrs. Collins?"

Mrs. Collins gave a chuckling little laugh and answered, "Well, I have enough coffee for breakfast, about a cup of oatmeal, one slice of bacon, a potato and a half, and some shoe polish."

They both laughed at her joke. Alice said that she had

thought they might unite their supplies and have a good meal, but shoe polish wouldn't go well with anything she had. "I wonder if the men who are batching up at the mine have anything we could borrow?"

"If you want cereal with the coffee you might borrow, for that with coffee was all they had for breakfast. Some of them have walked [the sixteen miles] to Globe. They'll be pretty hungry by the time they get there."

Tom came in, saying, "I was going to Globe for groceries, but some of the men are going with me to meet Hayden's wagon. It is stuck in the mud in Dripping Springs Valley, with a load of flour from Hayden's Mill in Tempe."

When the men returned late that night they brought flour from the Hayden's wagon, and sugar and coffee from Idaho Bill's ranch. They were saved from starvation! [The] next day the stage brought everything they needed. The road was repaired.

Tom had rigged up something he called a jigger, to sort ore. Black Jack Newman offered him five dollars a day to build one for him. Tom wrote to Duryea, telling him about it and [saying] that he would like to get this cash, as they would need clothes for the winter. Duryea answered at once, telling Tom to take the job, that he knew they needed some money.

After the jigger was working, Black Jack came to the Curnows' house and offered Tom three dollars a day for his labor, which Tom refused. Alice had been watching Black Jack's face, which took on a most villainous look. She called Tom into the bedroom and begged him to accept anything Black Jack offered. She was afraid of him. Tom reluctantly agreed, saying he would never again work for Black Jack.

This man was, Alice believed, a Hungarian, with an unpronounceable name. To overcome this difficulty, when he first came to the [United States], his bosses called him "The New Man," which finally became Newman. Another custom was to call one "Jack" whose name the boss couldn't remember, and to distinguish Newman from other Jacks, he became "Black Jack," from his complexion.

Black Jack Newman had some very valuable claims, which he leased to Mexicans with the agreement that they should have half of all ore taken out. Several Mexicans worked with this understanding, but when the ore was sacked and divided and ready to be shipped, Black Jack would take the ore belonging to the Mexicans and put sacks of sand in their places. He always expressed surprise that, while he received a generous check for his share of the ore, the Mexicans' ore was always worthless.

One group of miners would leave, but there were always others who were willing to try their luck, with the same result.

Two white men, Jack Eaton and Jim Evans, also had a lease from Black Jack, on the same terms as the Mexicans, but their lease proved worthless. Before leaving, they put up a job on Newman, knowing how he had treated the Mexicans.

[The men] knew he was watching them. [They] filled sacks with sand and had Idaho Bill, who did freighting, come up from Dripping Springs Valley late at night. They loaded the sacks of sand into his freight wagon, and then [he] stealthily drove away.

Black Jack immediately went to Globe, got the sheriff, and stopped Idaho Bill just as he reached his own home. The sheriff made him bring the sacks of sand back to Globe, the county seat, for trial.

After hearing the evidence, the judge decided that if Evans and Eaton wanted to ship sacks of sand and were willing to pay for it, it was nobody's business. And the case was dismissed, Black Jack having to pay the costs of court. Everyone in the courtroom jeered and laughed at Black Jack, who was generally disliked.

E.F. Kellner and Black Jack Newman. *Arizona Historical Society/Tucson, #50674.*

In a rage, Newman drew a pistol and fired at Jim Evans, who ran from the courtroom. Black Jack followed, shooting until he struck Evans in the arm. It had to be amputated to save the man's life.

Feeling ran high, and someone suggested lynching Black Jack. But Alonzo Bailey, who owned the largest general store in town and with whom Black Jack did business, said that he would shoot the first man that pulled on the rope, and the lynching [party] was over. Black Jack was sent to the penitentiary, from which he was pardoned in a short time. He was successful in money matters and died a very rich man.

The winter [of 1886] in Pioneer was terrible. The days were so short and the nights were long and cold. It snowed so much, and the fine snow sifted through the cracks in the walls that were protected only by battens, leaving "scarfs" of snow on the kitchen floor every morning. Although two rooms on each end of the building protected them, the cold was dreadful.

Alice did up her kitchen work with a roaring fire in the cook stove, which had no effect on the temperature. She dressed little Alice and Charles in their coats and hoods, and for a time they were satisfied to pretend that they were going for a ride on the chairs. But it was hard to keep up this deception indefinitely. Alice was afraid to trust them alone in the papered room, which a sheet iron stove made very comfortable. They might fall against it or tip it over. They had so little room to play in there!

Alice placed an armchair with its face toward the wall, its back toward the stove, to which it was very near. It had a very low back, with rungs all around the back and arms, through which the baby's feet were passed. With pillows about him and dressed very warmly, she managed to keep him from freezing to death.

The diapers that were hung before the open door of the oven, often froze. Then as the fire grew hotter they usually dried before night. Alice hurried with her work and managed to stay in the papered room during the afternoon. They ate in there, the children off chairs and she and Tom off the chest of drawers.

In February they had a dreadful snowstorm. Alice tried to persuade Tom to stay home, but he laughed at her, saying, "I couldn't fall off the trail *up* the hill. There is a bank on one side and a pile of dirt on the other. I will come home before dark, and you have plenty of wood and water in the house. So cheer up."

What a day it was! Alice couldn't see across the road, and [she] had no hope of seeing the stage, [usually] her only exciting happening for the day. She didn't dare let the children into the kitchen that day, but [she] left the door open into the "papered room," as they always called it. Having a papered room was a great luxury in Pioneer.

When the time came for Tom to come home Alice tried to see through the fog of snow, but the trail was invisible. At last she heard him trying to open the door. She ran to help him and he staggered in, saying, "You were right. I should have stayed home today. I'm nearly frozen."

Alice dished up on the kitchen table and they ate in the papered room. My, but it was nice and warm in there! It was surprising how happy warmth could make you feel on a cold day.

They had just finished their dinner when Alice thought she could hear someone calling. She opened the door. Someone *was* calling, but she couldn't tell from where [the call] came. It might have been from the sky as far as directions could be judged!

Tom called, "Hello" several times, and the stage driver straggled into the house.

"My horse," he said, as he fell into the armchair.

Tom, who was warm by then, went out and attended to the horse, while Alice got hot coffee for the man. He revived and said, "I couldn't have gone much farther. Lucky you folks heard me." Then suddenly he [uttered], "Wonder where I left the mail?"

Tom came in just then bringing the mail sack, saying, "Now, take it easy. You can't go any farther tonight."

They got the driver's coat off and he sat by the stove until Alice got something for him to eat. Tom fixed up a bed for him in the kitchen with horse blankets and whatever warm coats and rugs they could find. [The driver] was just leaving the room when he turned back. He took a letter from his pocket and handed it to Tom. "By George, I forgot this."

Tom opened it and read an invitation to go back to Globe. Walker had been put in charge of the Old Dominion Mine; [it was opening again].

The warmth of the fire didn't compare to the warmth of

their hearts as they began early the next morning to pack their things to move back to Globe. But when? The storm had passed, but the wind was still blowing drifts of snow into the road. Tom would go out every few minutes and look up toward the Pinals, but they couldn't be seen through the clouds.

As night came on the wind subsided, and next morning the sun was breaking through the clouds and the Pinals had appeared again: an omen of the good luck that was to be theirs.

The Curnows knew that if it were possible, the mail would go through, but it was late afternoon before the horseman arrived with word that it would be several days before the stage could travel.

Those were three of the longest days Alice ever lived. Nothing interested them but the condition of the road. Although the mountains presented a glorious sight of sparkling snow and frost on every tree and twig, Tom and Alice were scarcely conscious of its beauty. A stage would, just then, be far lovelier, even if it had neither springs or top.

Alice's sister Mary [Starr] had moved to Florence, so the Curnows went to a hotel in Globe until their furniture would come the next day. Tom went down to see the Scholefield family. Alice put the children in bed and then sat and listened to the occupants of rooms on each side of her singing. On one side a youth whom she thought must have been in love played on a guitar and sang:

> Pull down the blind, pull down the blind
> Somebody's looking, Love, don't be unkind.
> Though we're alone, bear this in mind
> Somebody's looking, Love, pull down the blind.

Sometimes the singer varied his music by singing

"Globe's Greatest Snowstorm," December 1898. *Arizona Historical Society/ Tucson, #61154, Gribble Collection.*

"Sweet Belle Malone," which was much more sad than "Pull Down the Blind." At the same time a woman on the other side was singing "Plant Green Roses on my Grave."

If they had sung one at a time it might not have been so bad, but with both singing at once Alice found it quite distracting. The man sang longest.

The Curnows rented a house with all the rooms lined and papered. The family all took colds, which they had escaped during their hardships in Pioneer.

When young Alice was seven years old [1888], her teeth were coming in very crooked, almost crosswise, and her parents were worried about it. At that time only a traveling dentist went to Globe periodically. He had filled the first tooth Alice [herself had] lost, a front one, seven times one summer, and the filling always dropped out. So she decided she should take her daughter to her mother's in Virginia City, Nevada, where she knew a child's specialist was practicing.

The stage left Globe at eight in the morning. Alice got

up very early to have her children [little Alice, Murray, and Charles] bathed, and breakfast over by that time. She made them sit on chairs in the bedroom with her, [so] that they wouldn't need another bath before they left, while she finished packing and strapping her bags and putting on her dress. Tom had gone to make some last-minute purchases for her.

Charles' little white woolly dog sat on the floor in front of the children, wagging its tail in evident surprise at their inaction. Then, springing to its feet, it crouched and barked at Charles as if challenging him to a race, which [challenge] the baby immediately accepted. As Alice had emptied the tub, and Charles couldn't open the door or get into any mischief by himself, she let him go while she entertained the other two by telling them of the adventures they were going to enjoy. She heard the dog give a peculiar bark, and she went to the kitchen to investigate.

At the door Alice stopped in amazement. The house had a chimney in the center, from which a fireplace [opened] into the living room in one corner of the house. Another [fireplace opened] into the kitchen in another corner. Having a piece of tin fitted to the opening had closed the latter, before which the cook stove was placed. The bottom of that tin had become bent outward slightly at one corner. Through this opening the dog had pushed, and Charles had followed.

Charles was a plump, roly-poly little boy with very fair skin, but when he and the dog emerged from that fireplace, there wasn't a white hair on the dog, or a white spot on Charles, except the whites of his eyes! Both were covered with soot. Alice tied up the dog and gave Charles another bath, which required a rinse this time. The stage had to wait for her.

Again Alice climbed the Pinal Mountains [with a baby on her lap], but this time she occupied the front seat, with springs. Young Alice and Murray sat in the back seat with the bags tied in such a manner they couldn't fall out.

Before they reached Florence, Alice noticed that the cottonwood trees along the bank of the Gila River were not only leafless, but also stark and white in the fierce sunlight. She asked the stage driver what had happened, and he said, "No water."

"What happened to the water?"

The driver shook his head. He wasn't interested. But a man seated beside her at the hotel dining table didn't need to be asked. He volunteered the information. "Did you notice our dead cottonwood trees along the Gila as you came into town?"

"Yes, what happened to your water?"

"A band of people came down from Utah, [went to Safford, and began farming. They dug ditches to divert Gila River water to their fields], and took [the water] away from the people of Florence and the Indians, who were farming when the first white man came to Arizona. They got their water from the Gila River. That should establish prior right to the water, but it didn't with the Government. It gave the water to the people of Safford. You will see the result all the way to the railroad."

"I don't understand. Why did the Government take the water away from the Indians?"

"Because old Mark [Marcus Aurelius] Smith[5] resigned as representative to fight the case for the Safford people. I suppose the Government thought the old rascal knew what was best for the people here."

Florence had lost its appearance of prosperity. The Silver King and other mines in the vicinity were closing. As they traveled along [toward Casa Grande], through the

---

5   [*Ed. Smith obtained the first reclamation appropriation of arid lands for the Safford area growers under the 1902 National Reclamation Act.*]

country that had been teeming with life the last time Alice had passed that way, everything was the picture of ruin. The fields had returned to the desert. Houses that had been abandoned, with windows missing, completed the scene of desolation.

The Curnow children had a glorious time [in Nevada]. Water in Virginia City and Gold Hill cost one dollar a week. If one had a tree or flowers, one paid more in proportion. Alice's mother had both. Among her flowers were some hollyhocks that she prized highly. She was planning to save all the seed. One morning Alice's father was sitting on the front steps reading the paper, and paying no attention to the children until he was ready to come in, when he called his wife.

He was decorated with those hollyhocks down his suspenders, front and back, in his beard, behind his ears—every place that a hollyhock would stick he carried one! His wife looked, but said never a word. There were no hollyhocks left in the garden.

At another time [while they were in Nevada], the sink in her parents' home was stopped up. Alice's father could usually clear the waste pipe that emptied into a canyon some distance from the house, with a long wire that he kept for that purpose. But that time the wire would go but a short distance. He discovered a spool driven tightly [into] the pipe. It had swelled from being in the water and he had to get a corkscrew to get it out.

He said, "Now turn the water on."

Young Alice volunteered, "There's another spool in there."

He had to cut the pipe before it could be cleared.

[*Ed. Mrs. Curnow did not mention two of her husband's ventures in 1888 while she and the children were visiting her parents. In June an advertisement appeared in the Globe newspaper for a meat market run by "Curnow & Co." It was taken over by James*

*Wiley in September. In October the paper reported that Curnow had
opened a carpenter shop in the Anderson Building at the corner of
Broad and Oak Streets, and that "he was expecting his wife and children home in a few days from Gold Hill, Nevada, where they have
been spending the summer with relatives."*]

When Alice returned to Globe, Tom was chief mechanic
at the Old Dominion Mine, and things [ran] smoothly for
them, although they were both working very hard. Alice did
all her own [house]work, and sometimes she did sewing for
her neighbors.

She saw an advertisement in the paper that a lot of
Globe's business street was to be sold for a thirty-five dollar
tax bill. She urged Tom to buy it.

"What for? For *me* to pay the taxes on it?"

"We could build a home there. It would be nearer to the
mine than where we are living, and just think! It is next to a
business block."

"But Alice, what would I build it with? We have no
money."

She kept dropping a seed occasionally that they were
paying twenty dollars a month for rent, when they might just
as well be paying it for a house of their own. At last Tom [pur-
chased a lot on the northwest corner of Bone and Broad
Streets and] made arrangements with Jerry Hyneman to fur-
nish the lumber and build a house of three rooms for two
hundred fifty dollars. The Curnows were to pay twenty-five
dollars a month and accept the house without lining, paper,
or paint.

[Their house] was on a corner without a fence, where
the cattle roamed at will. Mexicans, on their way home after
spending the evening enjoying themselves in some saloon,
would nearly always stop and argue loudly [in Spanish], and
rest. They leaned against the house for support (usually
under Alice's bedroom window), and sang.

They chorded harmoniously, but the end of each line or phrase was prolonged, until it ended in a wail that was heart-rending. Alice, too, wanted to cry aloud. Then, with a suddenness that was startling, the Mexicans began joyously to sing the next line, only to repeat the agony.

Alice was preparing dinner one afternoon when one of these warblers climbed her front steps and calmly went to sleep on her front porch. He had been there but a few minutes when Glenn Reynolds, their new sheriff, came, yanked the man to his feet, and led him away.

At last, they had an officer who would make people obey the law! Reynolds was a big, broad-shouldered man from Texas, and, while he was a heavy drinker, he made everyone a law-abiding citizen. "Either stay in the saloon or go home, or I'll put you in jail," were his orders.

There were several talented musicians in Globe at that time. Ed Lyons frequently put on entertainments with local talent that were very enjoyable. Tom Curnow was always the doorkeeper on these occasions, [held at the skating rink], as he was a good collector [of admissions].

There were two young men in town, whose names Alice chose not to mention, who always tried to beat their way into a show or dance. The method of one of them, later a prominent businessman of Globe, was to offer a twenty-dollar gold piece for the one-dollar entrance fee. He came early, before Tom would have collected that amount, when he couldn't make change.

One night Tom prepared himself by having twenty dollars in silver, nineteen of which this youth had to carry around with him the rest of the evening. The next time he brought a dollar.

A road show came to town and everyone attended. Tom, as usual, was doorkeeper. There was a commotion at the door. [Sheriff Reynolds] appeared to be pulling someone,

Skating Rink in Globe, Arizona, 1885. Tom Curnow on the right. *Arizona Historical Society/Tucson, #13774.*

much against his will, into the hall. The sheriff was having trouble persuading whoever it was to come to the show.

Reynolds braced himself against the doorframe on the inside, and his "victim," protested vigorously by bracing himself against the outside of the doorframe. When he was finally forced by the officer to enter, those about the door were amazed to see that he was handcuffed to the sheriff, who had been drinking heavily for several days.

The prisoner's tousled black hair and heavy black moustache gave him a criminal appearance. His black eyes flashed from one to the other of those standing about. Evidently he did not know what was to be done with him. A trial or a hanging?

The sheriff yanked him up to the table where the tickets were sold and purchased three: one for himself, one for his prisoner, and one for his deputy. The prisoner wiped beads of perspiration from his forehead as, with a look of relief upon his face, he willingly accompanied the officers.

Tom Curnow touched Reynolds on the shoulder and asked, "Who is this man, Glenn?"

"I arrested him this afternoon for murder, and I'm holding him for the sheriff from San Antonio. He'll be here tomorrow or next day."

"But why didn't you leave him in jail?" Tom asked.

"'Cause he looked so damned lonesome setting there in that little dark adobe jail, ('cause I don't leave no light in there 'cept a lantern hanging outside the barred windows) that I brung him erlong. 'Twas some job to bring the pup, too. Seemed t'like the old jail after all, but I thought he'd like the show after he'd got here."

The sheriff, accompanied by the deputy, led his captive to a seat and the show began.

A very stout, short, middle-aged lady came upon the stage, dressed in light blue satin trimmed with ruffles of flimsy white material; a crown of silver paper studded with jewels; and rings, bracelets, and strings of diamonds that, if real, would have bought an empire.

As she sang, "Whose Little Girl Are You?" she appeared to bounce about the stage in short, quick steps, while her long train, with ruffles flying, made frantic efforts to keep up with her, sometimes being in the lead. When this occurred she turned about, leaving [the train] in the rear.

No prima donna ever received more applause, to which she responded several times. Other equally successful performers appeared until eleven o'clock, when the audience departed, made happy by an evening's entertainment, for which it was hungry.

❧

Chapter Seven

Tom went for the paper every evening. One night he came home very indignant.

"Another teamster and his helper have been murdered, [their] mules stolen or killed, and two freight wagons with their contents have been burned by the Apaches. It's a shame the way [that] the Government agents are treating us. They arrest the Indians, keep them in jail for two or three months, then let them out and they commit the same crimes over again."

"I thought they were to be turned over to the civil authorities now."

"That's what we are trying to have done, but the bill hasn't been signed. Perhaps this will hurry it along, for there has been a great loss in that freight."

Tom was right. The bill was signed, and nine Indians were turned over to Gila County authorities. They were all convicted. One was hanged and the others were sentenced to terms in the penitentiary in Yuma.

The sheriff was given permission to call for soldiers from San Carlos to help conduct the Indians to the prison, but Reynolds said that if there was any glory in it, he wanted it himself. They left Globe on the stage, Eugene Middleton driving, with one Mexican prisoner, the eight Indians, and one deputy sheriff named Holmes.

[*Ed. Alice specifically recalled the day The Apache Kid killed Sheriff Reynolds*]. It was late in November. The day was overcast with clouds, indicating a storm, which materialized the next day in a snowstorm that occasionally turned to sleet. It was bitterly cold. A day she had cause to remember, as all the children were suffering from a slight rash that the doctor pronounced German measles, with orders to keep them warm.

Tom had wanted to hang the doors and put up the warming stove, but as the weather had been mild and Alice was anxious to have the house papered, this was done [first]. So when the sudden cold snap came, it was impossible to keep the house warm with just the cook stove, and so she kept the children in bed, much against their will. They had kept her busy supplying their wants, first at one bed [and] then the other, until she was glad when it was time for them to go to sleep.

Tom went for the mail and brought the news: Reynolds, with his prisoners, had spent the night in Riverside, from where they started early [the] next morning. [They rode] through rolling hills until they came to a nine-mile sand wash, when Middleton ordered the Indians to walk, [because] the team couldn't haul them.

Riverside Stage Station where The Apache Kid was held prisoner. *Arizona Historical Society/Tucson, #16205.*

All got out of the stage except the Mexican [prisoner]. They traveled in the following order: Reynolds, with his overcoat on and buttoned up, with his pistol in an inside pocket and gloves on; next came the Indians, handcuffed in pairs; and Deputy Holmes in the rear with a sawed-off shotgun.

The Indians were conversing in their own language. Evidently at a signal, two of them turned on Holmes, striking him with their handcuffs, killing him, and taking his keys. They unlocked their handcuffs while the others attacked Reynolds, who had been very severe with them. He thought he had cowed them.

The prisoners expressed their hatred by mutilating Reynolds so badly that he couldn't be seen at his funeral. Eugene Middleton was shot and fell out of the stage, where he "played possum" and survived. The Mexican whipped up the horses and drove to Florence, where he gave the alarm. He was [later] pardoned.

Indian trailers were brought from San Carlos. They trailed the prisoners to the top of a hill, where they separated. They were all accounted for by being killed, except for The Apache Kid, a graduate of [the Indian School at] Carlisle, Pennsylvania. For years he murdered isolated farmers and travelers.

"The Kid" would go to the reservation and take a young [woman], who had to cook and work for him until she was worn out, when he would kill her. Some [women] he turned loose. One of the latter told how "The Kid" would watch from the top of a mountain, with field glasses that he had taken from one of his victims. When he saw a horseman coming, he waited until the man was near enough to kill. The Apache Kid would then take the horse if it was better than the one he was riding, take whatever he fancied from his victim, and in this way he was always well supplied.

The Apache Indians were in deadly fear of "The Kid." Alice hadn't heard of any of his depredations in years, and supposed him to be dead.

❦

Tom wanted to buy a horse for the children, but Alice objected. She was afraid they might be thrown and hurt. Tom said that he knew just how badly the children wanted one, because he and John, his brother, wanted a horse when they were boys and never had one.

"That may be the reason neither of you ever had a broken arm or leg, as you have told me. Not yet, Tom. They are such little boys."

Nothing more was said about a horse, until one day Alice saw Tom coming up the road from work. She went to the kitchen to dish up the dinner. Tom didn't come in for such a long time that she looked out again to see him talking, much of [the conversation] in sign language, to an Indian. He appeared to be giving the measurements for something, and, pointing at the boys, he held up three fingers.

Murray and Charles were standing beside their father and [they] seemed very much excited. They danced first on one foot, then on the other, while they eagerly watched their father wave his arms in earnest conversation. They looked so happy that Alice knew the discussion was not about war. So she didn't interrupt the conference.

When Tom and the boys came in, Alice asked what was the excitement about.

Tom said, "You'll have to wait a few minutes and we'll show you."

The children were so excited that they ate very little, which was unusual. They followed their father out into the back yard. Alice was washing the dishes when Tom called her. She went out to see the children riding on an Indian pony. As it walked up over a little rise in the road, the children all slipped off over its hind legs, and the pony waited patiently until they had all mounted again.

Tom asked, "Well, are you afraid to have them own this steed?"

"No, it has been subdued as well as the Indians."

The Curnows didn't have that gentle little horse very long. Tom traded it for a better and more spirited one, but by that time the children could ride very well. The boys rode double, and young Alice had a ride every other day [after school]. Then one of the boys would go after their father at the mine, quite a long distance from town.

Tom continued trading horses until they had a fine carriage horse that called for a buggy. Then they all were happy.

❧

Rose and Nan Pendleton, classmates of young Alice, were spending the weekend with her. It was Sunday morning and they were dallying over breakfast. Alice usually had something extra for breakfast [on Sunday] for which she didn't give the time to prepare on school days. That morning it was hot cakes, of which [the children] were very fond.

Murray, who was always growing out of his clothes and seemed all legs like a young colt, came running into the house very much excited, and shaking his finger at the girls he said, "What do you think? Bean Walker's married!"

If Murray had announced that the town was on fire, it wouldn't have caused a greater sensation. The children dropped their knives and forks and sat in speechless wonder for a moment. Rose recovered first and asked, "Who'd she marry?"

"A man named Starr."

They still seemed rather stunned by the news, when Rose turned to young Alice and said, "Alice, I bet Bean Walker isn't more than three years older than you." (Alice was nine, going on ten.)

Another pause.

"And she's in my class," said Murray, who was the youngest in the group, except Charles. "And Friday the teacher told her that if she didn't do better work she'd have to go back into the baby class. She doesn't know anything."

"Well, she knows enough to get married," said Rose, who could always be depended upon to take the other side of any question. "I suppose she thinks we'll call her Mrs. Starr! Well, I won't. When I meet her I'll just pass by as I always do and I'll say 'Hello, Bean.'"

Another plate of hot cakes on the table stopped the conversation for a moment. Then Rose said, "Alice, let's walk down past Bean's house, and if she is out in the yard, or if she comes out, we'll say 'Hello, Bean.'"

They returned from the walk without any result. The only other sensation Bean Walker ever caused [in Globe] was when she filed papers for a divorce.

❧

The Curnows' evening meal was always interesting. It was the only time they didn't hurry. The children had some school news, and Tom wanted to know how the horse was behaving. After dinner the children looked over their lessons while Tom went for the mail.

The children were sometimes given the class papers to correct, and each had their favorites. When it was young Alice's turn, she talked aloud, "Rose Pendleton. I'll give her 95. (Murray was listening attentively.) Willie Crampton, 75."

Willie was Murray's favorite schoolmate, and a very bright boy, so Murray resented this grade. "Willie is the best student in our class!"

The only notice young Alice gave his remark was to repeat, "Willie Crampton, 75."

"All right, when it's my turn to correct the papers, I'll give old Rose Pendleton 50!"

This brought on a lively discussion, in which Alice joined. She persuaded young Alice to read Willie's paper carefully and give him his just grade, which she did.

Schooling was a serious problem for the parents. Nearly every year they had a new teacher. No grades were given. Each teacher employed the same method to place the pupils where they belonged: The whole school, young and old, were given examples in addition. Those who gave prompt and correct answers for a week or more were advanced to subtraction, and so on, until everyone was in his or her proper place. This took so much time that it was quite late in the term before everyone was placed. One young woman told Alice that because of this method, she never passed fractions.

One morning Alice was combing and braiding young Alice's lovely brown hair. The style was to braid in two parts, cross [them] in the back, and tie [them] with a brightly colored ribbon over the ears. Alice had nearly finished one braid when young Alice said, "We had a lot of fun in school yesterday. Will Shanley left his seat without permission, walked across the room and took a drink of water. Then he stood [there] saying, 'Ah-a-a-ah-a-ah.'

"Mr. Duffy said, 'Will Shanley, sit down!' Will looked up as if he were surprised and said, 'Will I sit down, Duffy? Will I sit down?'

"Then he took another drink of water and said, 'Ah-a-a-ah-a-ah,' then he danced a little and walked over to Tom McKevit's desk. He looked at Tom's book and smiled at Mr. Duffy, saying, 'Well, I guess I will sit down now, I'm tired.'"

Young Alice was quite thrilled with this show of independence. Alice was astonished at this show of lack of discipline.

"We are going into fractions today," Young Alice announced.

"Has the class finished this page of miscellaneous

examples?" Alice asked. "Oh, yes! We finished that page last Friday."

[Her arithmetic book] was lying open at that page [of examples]. Alice read the first example about a man in a boat, rowing upstream a certain number of feet per minute. The current carried him back a few feet less per minute. How long would it take him to reach a certain distance?

Young Alice looked startled, and then answered, "I didn't get that one."

Alice read the next [one] and she sullenly answered, "I didn't get that one either."

The same answer was given until Alice came to the fifth [example], when her daughter brightened and answered, "No one in the class got that one."

And so it continued to the bottom of the page.

"But we are going into fractions today," she announced.

"No, my dear, you are going to stay home and study."

Alice sent Murray to her sister who was living in Mesa, and both the children did well in their studies that year.

※※※

It was two days before Christmas in that year of 1891. Alice had been unusually busy. She had everything ready for that extra bed that she knew they would need, except to tack one corner of a comforter that she was making.

She went for a bucket of water, and in her hurry she let go of the rope with one hand before she had quite clasped it with the other. Her hand was drawn up into the wheel and her thumbnail was turned back, hurting her dreadfully. But she managed to finish the comforter and prepare the dinner.

After everyone was asleep that night, Alice read in a San Francisco paper the full account of Ruth Cleveland's layette. It included a silver trimmed baby buggy! She went to bed about eleven o'clock and their daughter, Helen, was born the next morning, [December 23, 1891].

It was near night before the excitement of the new baby's arrival settled down to normal. Tom came into the bedroom and asked, "Where are the things for the children?"

"What things?"

"For Christmas. Have you forgotten that this is Christmas Eve?"

Alice had forgotten all about it! "What shall we do?" she asked.

"Do! Why, I'll have to buy something for them."

And he bought everything in sight. Among other things he found a house for young Alice. When the front gate was opened, the curtains on all the windows rolled up and a paper doll appeared at every opening. She had the best time! By the time Alice was about again the dollhouse needed a thorough repairing.

Tom found a bottle of perfumery that looked like a tiny bottle of wine, in which was a tiny doll. Young Alice managed to spill the perfumery, but the doll was still too large to come out, so she placed the bottle under the rocker of the chair in which Alice was sitting, and it was Alice who released the doll. Young Alice had other dolls, but this one was very desirable.

The officers from San Carlos often played baseball with the Globe men, many of whom were college men working in the mine, clerking in stores, or doing anything they could find to do [for the summer]. These games always took place on Sunday.

Tom wanted to attend but was, Alice thought, loath to leave her at home. This was no hardship for her, as she knew nothing about the game, but Tom insisted that she go, [saying] he would stand beside her and explain every play. He carried the baby, Helen, and a folding chair for his wife. No seats were provided, nor was any admission charge made, as the ball ground was an open field.

"The Athletics" of Globe, baseball team. *Arizona Historical Society/Tucson, #61151.*

Tom found a good place to see the game, which had just begun, so a man told them. Alice was "all set" to learn baseball.

The batter sent the ball flying and the players ran madly about, but she couldn't tell where they were trying to go. One moment they were running in one direction and again in another, and throwing the ball to someone, again falling in a group on top of it.

Tom was so busy shouting and clapping his hands and congratulating anyone who would listen to him, that he had no time to tell Alice the cause of his joy until they were coming home. He asked, "Did you see Doc make that home run?"

"Was he trying to go home?" she asked.

"No, no. He *made* a home run just at the end of the game and the home team won."

As people passed them they would slap Tom on the shoulder and laugh wildly and tell each other that it was a great game. It must have been, [Alice thought], for everyone was so madly happy. That was her last lesson in the Great American Game.

San Carlos Apaches drawing rations, 1880s. *Arizona Historical Society/ Tucson, #22295, Wood Collection.*

❦

In March of each year, when the worst of the winter was over, the agency at San Carlos issued rations of bedding and clothing to the [Apache] Indians, which they immediately took to Globe to sell. The only medium of exchange they seemed to know was one silver dollar. This was the price of the following articles: a woolen overshirt; a pair of shoes; [an] excellent gray army blanket with "U.S." woven in the center in a darker color; a sateen-covered comforter; and five yards of dark blue twill flannel. After a time they became shrewder and tore the flannel into two pieces, asking one dollar for each.

When everything had been disposed of, the Indian men gathered in back of the Curnows' house on a vacant lot, where the neighborhood children played baseball. They gambled with Mexicans, and some white men, until all their money was gone, after which they were always present in time to collect the money earned by the [Indian women] in a hard day's work of washing. Then the poor [woman] lifted her baby in its basket [to her back], supported by a strap across her forehead. She trudged away, only to repeat her profitless labor the following day.

As time passed, the g-string style of dress was discarded. The Indian men adopted overalls and shirt. At first no hats were worn; these came later. The women, a style they were still following in 1934: A very full [gathered] skirt of red or blue calico with small white figures. A ruffle [on the bottom], six to twelve inches wide, also very full, was trimmed with several narrow bands of various plain-colored calicos. The waist was a plain yoke sewn onto a very full bottom hanging loose. Some of the yokes [were] trimmed with bands like the ruffle and some [were] plain. All had full sleeves

Apache Women in traditional dress. *Arizona Historical Society/Tucson, #50619, PC 122, Box 1, page 2.*

gathered into a band at the wrists, beaded if possible, but no hat.

This style never varied. As the Indian [woman] acquired a new dress, it was put on over the old one. All her wardrobe was carried on her back. As she walked along the road her skirts swung in great ripples about her. Apparently the greater the ripple, the more stylish she was.

Alice had read that the progress of a people is indicated by the changing styles of its women. She believed the Apache [woman] bore out this fact: There was no progress here.

The Government built pretty little houses on the reservation, painted them white, and turned them over to the Indians. The only use they made of the houses was to put their saddles, bridles, plows, and farming utensils in them. [The Indians] slept outside as usual. Undoubtedly, [Alice thought, they] found it healthier, as many Americans do.

One Christmas in Miami [Arizona], many years later, Alice saw an Indian man looking at a cut glass candlestick in a jewelry store. He then went outside and tried to pull a [woman] into the store, but she pulled away from him and refused to even look at it. Perhaps she was wise. It might not have matched anything in her [wickiup]!

⁂

The winter rainy season usually began in December, sometimes as early as November. But [in 1891] it was February before they had any rain at all. The grass had dried up and no water had been running in Pinal Creek for months.

The cattle had all gone to the hills, where even there the water holes had to be made deeper, and the cattlemen were kept busy cleaning them out. Everyone was affected by the drought, mentally if not financially, seeing their neighbors who had been prosperous, reduced to such straits, driving herds to new ranges and desperately trying to develop water supplies. It was so discouraging! Not a cloud in the sky until early in February.

Then it began to rain in the mountains, then turned to snow, driving the stock from the hills and feed to the valleys where there was nothing for them to eat. The Pinals were again covered with snow when it turned to rain again, sending a torrent of water down the [Pinal] creek. Again it snowed in the hills, but by that time the rain was sending water from every canyon, until it flooded the town of Globe in back of the stores.

The Curnows watched from the surrounding hills while the snowstorm in the mountains again turned to rain, swelling the water in the creek until it was bank full and rising every moment.

The footbridge that crossed the creek where it turns sharply east and crosses Globe's Broad Street had withstood the strain [while] twenty-one houses had been undermined and toppled into the stream. Debris from the houses piled up against the bridge, when, with a crash heard above the roar of the water, it went out in the pitchy darkness of that February night.

For three weeks that storm continued, without the sun shining even for a moment. It had become a nightmare.

The Curnows' house stood behind the hill where the creek turned east. They were in no danger, but to hear the crash of the falling houses drove sleep away. The flood continued for so long that Alice was walking from one window to another, although she could see nothing in the blackness of the night.

She could hear people shouting below them, where a very pretty white house with green blinds stood on the bank of the creek, but back far enough, so she thought, to be in no danger. Alice went out on the front porch and could see lanterns being swung wildly about, and that house was all

Pascoe's Corral, 1891 Flood. *Arizona Historical Society/Tucson, #73754.*

lighted up. Suddenly, with a crash, [the house] disappeared.

In the morning they heard that the owner [of the pretty white house] had taken a lantern to see how far his house was from the creek, only to find that it was hanging over the water. The shouts Alice had heard were his, when he shouted to his family to get out, which they did just in time to save their lives.

❧

At that time the grand jury met in Florence, where there was very little business. To help this situation, prospective members of the jury were often summoned ten days or two weeks before court convened, and many more men were summoned than could possibly act.

This was a great hardship, for some of the men could ill afford to lose the time [from work]. On one occasion, to retaliate, several of them thus called continued on to Phoenix, where they remained until court proceedings began.

To avoid this unnecessary absence from work, Tom

Curnow joined the militia. He was in charge of putting a big pump in the sump of the mine, and just at that time [he] couldn't very well be spared. After this work was finished, he remained with the militia. He was interested in the work and Alice never thought of his being called to active duty. In fact, she thought nothing about it [at all].

They read in the papers of the great railroad strike in the East.

"Of course it couldn't affect us," the Curnows told themselves.

They were sometimes amused at the account of some rich woman going to the armory, demanding that her husband be released as he was "a businessman, and very wealthy." Yes, it was very amusing when it occurred in Baltimore or Philadelphia, but as [the strike] traveled west and reached St. Louis, the prospects of their immunity from its effects were not so assuring.

"The coke in the freight wagons on the road from Willcox is all we will have until this strike is over," Tom said one night.

"Will that shut down the mine?"

"Certainly. [We] must have coke to run the smelter."

Alice was to know more anxiety than the closing [of the mine] before that strike was over, [but for the moment] it passed Arizona [and went] into California. Not only coke, but also other supplies began to disappear, and they were faced with the possible shortage of food.

Tom had gone to the armory one night when Mrs. X called on Alice to tell her, "The regulars have been called from San Carlos, and the militia will have to take their places, and follow them up if this trouble grows. Mr. X just heard about it, and I thought that you should know. The men are preparing at the armory right now. They will leave very early in the morning."

Alice was glad when [Mrs. X] left her. She wanted to be

alone. She was terribly frightened. Perhaps it might end in war. The children were eagerly asking questions, which she could not answer. Alice went into the bedroom and took Tom's things out of the bureau drawer. She wondered if there would be another Indian uprising while he was in the Army, and [if] he would have to fight them, too.

His underwear, of course he would need that, but what about overshirts? She was folding and unfolding the things and having a despairing weeping spell, when one of the X children came to tell her that the strike was over. By the time Tom came home, Alice and the children had recovered their spirits and were singing to welcome him.

꧁꧂

Chapter Eight

After finishing her housework, Alice would take her mending out on the vine-covered porch. Helen always joined her in her little rocking chair, getting as close to Alice as possible, then demanding a story. She had many committed to memory from repetition for the other children.

Then when it came Helen's turn [to tell] a story, she always gave the same one: "There was a little dog and he bit his little leg." The other children objected to Helen always giving the same [Bible] verse, "Till He cometh," in Sunday school.

Alice never bothered teaching her children their letters or anything other than what they learned by association, in the years before school age. [In this way] they learned the language and the names of objects.

When asked her name Helen would answer, "Papa's boy, Mother's sweetheart, and Helen to everyone else."

She was a very pretty child with fair skin, very dark blue eyes, and lovely soft golden-brown hair that curled over Alice's fingers as she combed it out. She was a lovable, gentle little girl, never aggressive. She seemed to know when it was time for Charles to return from school, for at that time she watched from the corner of the fence, and when he appeared she ran to meet him.

[Helen] met her father in the same way, and he always lifted her before him up in the saddle, from where she called, "See, I'm driving."

⁘

Alice was cleaning a turkey [one November day in 1895]

when Tom came in from work. As he put his lunch bucket down he said, "Thanksgiving, huh? Where did you get it?"

"From a peddler who comes in from Safford. Charlie is riding about town with him. I have some fresh butter and eggs, too."

"That's fine, but it has turned so cold, what do you say to going to the Pascoe Restaurant for Thanksgiving dinner? They are sure to have a good one, and [you can] cook our turkey on Sunday."

"All right. It will keep, I am sure, [as] it has turned so cold."

The family enjoyed their dinner at Pascoe's, then walked along the three blocks of [Globe] that had sidewalks. It was a glorious moonlit night. When they arrived home Alice played [the piano] and the children sang until bedtime.

Charlie wakened his mother in the night, asking if he might come into her bed. He was feverish, and Alice, thinking that he had eaten something that didn't agree with him, gave him a dose of castor oil. He slept fitfully the rest of the night.

She was surprised that he wanted to come into her bed, as he was a brave, manly little fellow. (Afterward Charles told her that he was frightened, that he could see crawlers in his eyes. Alice always wondered if it could have been possible for Charles to see the germs that had attacked him.)

Morning found the child still in a high fever. Alice sent for Dr. Collins, who pronounced it as typhoid, of which Globe had an annual epidemic, [resulting in] many deaths. "I have this case in time to check it, said the doctor, "If you will see that he gets the medicine and that he eats nothing but milk."

"I will follow your orders." She was afraid to trust Charles with anyone else but herself, so she sat up with him Saturday night, when Tom urged her to go to bed. He [said he] would sit up and give the medicine at a certain time. When that time came Alice was wide-awake.

So she continued the watch, and by Sunday morning Charles' fever was gone. She still insisted on the milk diet. When the poor child saw her coming with a glass of milk, the tears streamed down his face and he assured her that he was not hungry. He said the milk burned his throat dreadfully. But Alice insisted on [it].

The next afternoon young Alice came staggering into the house, unable to undress [herself]. She blamed her first corset waist, which she had worn for the first time that day, for her condition. Alice helped her undress and again called Dr. Collins. He said young Alice was suffering from tonsillitis, and [he] ordered a spray [for her throat]. She wanted nothing to eat, which the doctor said was just as well.

That afternoon Alice was, so she thought, ill with both their diseases. She could describe it only by the feeling that her flesh was being torn apart, and her throat was dreadfully sore. She sat very close to the fire, for she was very cold. Helen, as usual whenever Alice sat down, drew her rocking chair up as close to her mother as she could.

Alice said quite crossly, "Don't come so close to me. I can't move."

Helen looked up at her through her pretty brown curls and said, "Don't talk hard to me. Don't you love your sweetheart?"

Alice was so ill she did not answer her. She stayed up to keep the fire burning until Tom came, for it was very cold. He came at last, helped her to bed, and gave Helen her supper. After putting Helen in bed, he went for medicine and to find a woman to stay with them. The next day he went to work as usual.

Alice kept Charlie and young Alice in bed with her, that she might keep them covered. This was hard to do; both were feverish and they had heat added to their suffering. Alice's temperature had gone down. She was glad that Murray was in Mesa with Mary, on account of the school.

The woman that Tom found was not very efficient. Alice could hear Helen ask for her dinner several times before she was waited on. "Will you swab my throat?" Alice would hear her ask, so she knew her throat was hurting her.

The woman had been using turpentine, without the doctor's knowledge, but as it seemed to relieve Helen, Alice said nothing about it. She sprayed her [own] throat night and day in an effort to get well before Helen was stricken with what she thought was a severe case of tonsillitis, to which the family was subject.

The woman charged five dollars a day, [and she] left as soon as Tom came home from work, not even waiting until he had gone to town to get whatever they needed. While he was gone, a neighbor came in and said that hot lemonade had helped her [with] a similar sore throat, from which she had just recovered. Alice didn't like to ask her to prepare some for the children, so after [the neighbor] had gone, Alice got up, heated water, and made lemonade for them. But it hurt their throats so badly they couldn't drink it.

Alice, who was getting better, had a relapse of whatever they had. She began to wonder what it was.

When Tom came home that night, bringing more spray and other medicine, he looked anxiously at them. He put his hand on Charles' head. Asking more particularly than usual about their symptoms, [he] said, "Doc says that you are all out of danger unless you take a relapse, and there is no necessity for you to get up until you can't have a relapse."

"You seem to know what we have; do you?"

"I'm afraid I do. The Heron baby died today of diphtheria."

"So that's what we have?"

"Yes. And to make you careful I had to tell you, because I knew if the children wanted anything you would get up. Now you know how important it is that you get well first.

"What I can't understand is, how did just the Heron

family and ours get this diphtheria, for we are the only ones in town who have it, the Heron family at one end of town and we at the other."

"Have the other Heron children taken it?" [Alice asked.]

"Yes, the other two are very low, not expected to live through the night. Of course you are all on the improve, so the doctor says. So go to sleep and rest easy."

"Poor Mrs. Heron. She wouldn't go anyplace so her children wouldn't take whooping cough or any contagious disease. Living away out there where there isn't a house near her. I wonder where we got it."

Next morning the woman who had been helping them refused to remain when she learned what they had. The doctor wired Mary to come to them. Over the King Trail it still required two days to come from Mesa to Globe. During those two days Tom had to do everything for his family, which kept him busy.

Helen followed her father about the house; she was lonesome. Occasionally she would ask, "Papa, would you swab my throat?" She didn't appear to be suffering like the rest of them, so far as Alice could judge. She was eating everything without the pain that it caused the others to swallow anything. It was like swallowing fire to even take a drink of water.

Alice was lulled into the hope that Helen had not yet contracted the disease. They had been careful to keep her out of the bedroom, although she would follow her father to the door. Reaching out her little arms to Alice, that [her own arms] were aching to clasp, [Helen] would ask, "Couldn't I come into your bed? You know I always liked your bed best."

Alice, who had lost her voice, would raise her open hand in protest. Helen's sad little face at this denial haunted her yet.

How relieved they were when Mary came on the

second day! She had left Murray with friends in Mesa. Helen was happy; she had company at last.

The Curnows were in quarantine, so Tom ordered a big ham [so] that he wouldn't be without meat if their guard should wander too far from their door. To keep this fresh, Tom hung it on their vine-covered back porch, where he had put other things for the same reason. Everything was stolen the morning after Mary came. The guard had wandered far that morning, making breakfast very late. They didn't mind; they were happy to be together.

The doctor told them that if they would scald their clothes in a tub and set it outside while it was still hot, he would find someone to do their washing. But no one would go near them. Although Tom was a member of the Odd Fellows and Knights of Pythias, they did nothing for them. The Curnows did not need financial help, but [they] were badly in need of physical aid. Everyone was afraid of them, so Tom took his place at the washtub.

After hanging the clothes on the line, he stood wagging his finger at the clothesline, then came in and proudly told [his family] how many pieces he had washed.

Mary had Alice's bed moved into the dining room, where the warming stove kept her more comfortable. At last she allowed Helen to come to her, as she could no longer sit up. She would lie down on the floor and immediately go into a heavy sleep. Still Alice didn't fear for Helen, [rationalizing], "She is having such a light case."

Young Alice and Charles had recovered to the extent that they were both up and dressed, and for once Alice didn't have to urge young Alice to practice. She was glad to do so. But Helen, who usually liked music, roused from one of those deep sleeps enough to shake her head in protest. Young Alice had to stop playing "Clayton's Grand March."

On the doctor's advice, Charles, warmly dressed, had

been allowed to go outside. Alice had not approved of this, but he was anxious to go and [she rationalized again], "The fresh air will do him good," so she consented. The wind off the snow on the Pinal Mountains was biting cold. Charles soon came back in, but not soon enough. He went back to bed.

Helen slept often that day, and each spell lasted longer. Mary remarked that she thought Helen's face was very gray, and wanted to waken her, but Alice said, "No, let her sleep. She will probably be better when she wakes up again."

But the child's waking spells grew shorter and shorter, although she sat up and took some milk at bedtime. She didn't disturb them that night. That was the first night Alice had slept well since Thanksgiving, but she wakened [on December 17, 1895], to find her baby dying, just one week before she would have been four years old.

The authorities ordered that Helen be buried that day. The undertaker brought her coffin, in which her father placed her body . He carried it to the wagon and [he] had to place it in her grave. When he came home after that ordeal he was quite overcome. It began to rain just at dark, making their loss even more poignant.

After Helen was taken from her bed, Alice noticed that Charles hadn't gotten up. She asked the doctor to examine him. "He's all right," was the report, given without going near the boy.

Alice managed to dress, and she found Charles with a high fever. He had evidently taken cold. The doctor was quite indignant to be called back before he had reached home, but this time he found Charles suffering from pneumonia. "Doctors think that mothers don't know, without a thermometer, when their children are sick, but we know that we do," [Alice declared].

Tom and Alice spent an anxious night putting on hot

applications and giving Charles a teaspoonful of brandy and one of chicken broth every hour, with orders to waken him for this nourishment. When the brandy turned his stomach, Alice stopped giving it to him, again calling down the wrath of that doctor upon her head. The brandy was a heart stimulant, but how was she to know without being told?

It was a long siege, but they won. Charles lived.

(In the fall of 1897, diphtheria again visited Globe, in isolated families. A boy of Charles' age died of the disease. The investigation that followed revealed that Safford had suffered an epidemic of diphtheria, where the peddler's wagon had served as a hearse. The boy who had died had ridden about town with the peddler, as Charles had done. Their dread of the disease was over when they could trace its source. The peddler was refused permission to ever again sell his wares in Globe.)

When she had recovered, Alice and the children moved to Mesa. It was February 1896. Tom visited them the following summer and bought a horse for the boys, on which they rode double and accompanied their father all over the valley.

[It amused Alice that] Tom could never find his way out of that town [Mesa] that was laid out in perfect squares. After riding about for an hour or two, he would frequently find himself at the same corner from which he had started. But in the mountains he could find his way to any place that he wanted to go. For this reason the boys, Charles (age 9) and Murray, "Twenty minutes to twelve," (Alice called each month five minutes) accompanied their father to the edge of the desert when he left for Globe, where the mining company had summoned him.

When the boys returned, Murray sat with his arms hanging down beside his chair, looking very sad and hot.

"What's the matter, Murray, are you sick?"

"No, but I think this is a dickens of a way to live, without a father."

Alice was startled. It was like children in a divorced family! She put her arms around him, but while he didn't repulse her, he didn't respond to her embrace. "Come, we'll have lunch now and talk over moving back to Globe," Alice said.

Murray's tears were dried and he jumped up to help her, while he asked all kinds of questions: When could they start? Could he take his horse? Everything was planned for their next move.

"First I must find someone to rent the house." Alice [hadn't been able to] find a house to rent in Mesa, and had bought one. Murray wanted to go out at once to find a tenant. He was a great help.

The piano had cost fifty dollars to take to Mesa. As things at the mine under a new administration were rather uncertain (the new manager was bringing in his own friends to fill the best positions), Alice didn't want to move it back to Globe. Nor did she want young Alice to be without practice, so she and the piano were left with Mary. Alice continued her study in music.

There were no [public] conveyances between Mesa and Florence, so Alice found a man who at one time had operated a stage line in that vicinity, and who would take them back to Globe.

To avoid the heat, they started one bright moonlit night to cross the desert to Florence. She thought it would be too hard on Murray to ride the horse, but as that was the only way the animal could be taken, Murray insisted he could do it. That night, every time he rode up beside the stage for company, a rattlesnake would frighten the horse [and it] would jump back into the road. Alice thought the boy must have had a very lonely ride, but he didn't complain.

Murray, who was very studious, found the Globe school

not so good as those in Mesa. On that account, he begged to return to Mary.

Tom's place [at the Old Dominion Mine] had been given to someone else that spring. His old company [The Silver Reef Mining Company], hired him as chief mechanic, at a good salary, and sent him [to the Peck Mine, fourteen miles southwest of Casa Grande] to put some machinery in one of their mines.

The morning Tom left Alice was very downhearted. She didn't know how long he would be gone, young Alice and Murray would be in Mesa until school closed, and she and Charles were alone.

The day before he left, a new neighbor moved into the house below them on the hill. Alice didn't know them, and didn't pay any attention to them, as she was busy preparing Tom for his journey.

He had just gone when Mrs. [Kate] Robertson, the new neighbor, called at Alice's back door. After introducing herself she asked to borrow a tub. She was a happy woman, always singing, and that day she sang all day long, giving a command to her children on the last note of each line in the following manner:

> We'll never say good-by in heaven,
> (Get out of mother's starch.)
> We'll never say good-by.
> (Let mother's clothespins alone.)
> For in that land of joy and song
> (Don't put dirt in mother's rinse water.)
> We'll never say good-by.
> (Don't put your bread and sugar on the hot stove.)

Alice had listened unconsciously to this, [making her] want to feel sorry for herself. So she locked her door and trekked to the top of "Boot Hill." Even there she couldn't keep her mind on her duty to be sad. "We'll never say good-by in heaven" had lifted her spirits above sadness, even in that graveyard.

Alice stayed until the middle of the afternoon, thinking that "Sister Katie" (as they who knew and loved her learned to call her) would be too tired after doing a big washing to still be singing. But as Alice opened her door, she was just finishing the last line, with this comment:

"We'll never say good-by. (If he hasn't starched Mother's stockens!)"

✥

Tom Curnow left Globe in April [1897 to work in the Peck Mine], and on July 17 the couple's last child, Frances, was born. She was four months old before her father saw her, after he had finished the work of placing the machinery in the mine near Casa Grande.

✥

[*Ed. The Old Dominion Mine was closing down again, unemployment in Globe was increasing, and the Curnows joined the migration to the Salt River Valley.*]

Tom and Alice decided to move to the Salt River Valley, where they hoped the children would have better schooling and where, out of their savings they bought twenty acres of land and a water share for one hundred fifty dollars.

Again, Alice rode in the stage up the Pinal Mountains holding a baby in her arms. This time, however, the older children were able to hold themselves on the seat of the stage, so the journey was not so tiresome.

The desert between Florence and Mesa was practically level. It had been a good year, with plenty of rain in the valley and a heavy fall of snow in the mountains. On the desert east of Mesa, beyond the Highland Canal that carried water only in time of flood, men with teams were putting in grain. So intent were they on their work that they answered the [stage] driver's wave of his hand with only a nod of the head.

They didn't waste energy in whistling or singing. [They only made] pleasant calls to their teams as they urged them on to greater effort.

The sky gave evidence of more rain, and [the farmers] must be prepared to use it when it came. One man, who afterwards was the Curnows' neighbor, made enough money on grain that year to build a brick house large enough to accommodate his family of twelve children.

⚜

Tom and Alice had been married more than eighteen years when they moved to Mesa, and they had gotten along very well. They were not "the ideal couple who never had a cross word," but nothing serious had ever come between them. They were too busy making a living and caring for their family.

Tom bought the interest of Charles Mullen in a blacksmith shop in Mesa, which was a mere shack on a side street. "It has a hole in the wall back of the forge big enough for a horse to go through," Tom told Alice.

His partner owned a lot on the main street. Tom urged

Fields in the Salt River Valley, c. 1900. *Sharlot Hall Museum Library/Archives, Prescott, Arizona. (PB 105, F. 4, I. 5.)*

him to build a good brick shop, and [he offered] to pay rent. This the man did, and they equipped [the new shop] with machinery and tools. [They] were doing very well, but Tom was getting irritable and cross. [He] was always telling Alice of something wrong the boys had done, which she never believed.

While [they were] in Globe, the Curnows never had much cash on hand. They were always paying on something. When the house was paid for, Alice sent for a piano for young Alice, which they paid for on the installment plan. Alice knew many people did not approve of this [financial arrangement], but she did.

When the installment and their living expenses were paid, there wasn't much left. It was put in the bureau drawer, to be used for incidental expenses. Tom had never questioned Alice on its use, but after going into the business he put the money from the sale of their home in Globe in the bank, saying, "I must have a checking account to do business."

Alice didn't object. When she asked for money Tom would bring it to her.

⁕

The year after they had moved on the ranch, where Tom had built a house, there was little rain in the Valley, or snow in the mountains. Each succeeding year for eight years this [water] supply grew less.

Murray and his mother were driving to Phoenix to do some shopping when he noticed a lot of [live]stock wandering around in a plowed field. He stopped the team to ask a man who was standing by the fence the reason.

"No feed," he replied, "So I've plowed up the alfalfa roots and the cattle are eating that now. I'm trying to keep them alive until it rains, if it ever does."

Alice noted that a few of the farmers and many of the

businessman in the Valley who, during those prosperous years, had been urging [the building of] a dam across the Salt River to conserve its short watershed supply, were now gaining attention. The Government was being petitioned to build the Roosevelt Dam.

George W.P. Hunt, [who had come to Globe in 1891], was in the [Territorial] Legislature at the time. He was opposing the dam. While Alice was in Phoenix she went to see him, to learn his reason for this stand. Here it is:

When the dam is built, the water of the lake, which it will create, will [submerge] all of Gila County's tax-producing farm property, [and preclude the building of a wagon road or a railroad connection to the north from Globe], without [the county] receiving any benefit for its loss. Hunt wanted power and lights for Gila County, and he said the people [in the Salt River Valley] wanted, not only all the water which Gila County couldn't get, but all the other benefits from the dam, which he thought was not just.

Many ranches in the area were of twenty acres, which yielded three crops of alfalfa and one of grain in the winter, when the alfalfa didn't grow. A twenty-acre farmer could hire [an itinerant] man with a mower, a header, and baling machines, with a crew of men (paid by the month and "found"[6]) to do this work cheaper than the farmer could afford to own such expensive machinery.

When one of these machines broke down, the expense of the crew went on until the machine was repaired. So when [a machine] was brought into the [blacksmith] shop, Tom Curnow got help and worked by candlelight, if necessary, to have that machine ready to go out the next morning. When his partner, a leading Mormon, received notice of a church

6 meals

meeting, he dropped everything and attended, no matter about the urgency of having the machine repaired. He always provided a helper, who was very inefficient. This method of doing business did not suit Tom.

Then too, the continued drought was crippling the farmers. One of them asked Tom to buy his grain crop that had just been harvested.

"What would I do with grain?"

"Make some money on it. I will let you have it for eighty-seven cents a sack, and it will go up just as soon as the bankers have taken it from the farmers [as payment] on the mortgages we must give every year for money to buy seed grain.

"These mortgages always come due when the grain is cut. It isn't like buying stock; you have the grain. If I can sell I will make a little on it, but if the mortgage takes it there will be nothing left for me."

"Did you say that this happens every year?"

"Yes."

"Then why do you plant grain if you make nothing on it?"

"Always hoping it will be better. One good year, with plenty of water, would give us a big profit. The crop this year is unusually poor on account of the drought. If you buy it, I will put it in the warehouse, have it insured, and bring the receipts to you."

"All right."

The farmer was right. Wheat went to over two dollars. Alice didn't remember just how much, but she did know it was [at least] that much.

As the summer advanced, cattlemen from the hills came into the Valley looking for pasture, without success. A survey had disclosed the fact that there was but three weeks' feed supply for their cattle of that section. A meeting was held [of the cattlemen] in Phoenix to discuss the situation, and a committee was sent to California to find pasture there.

[One day] Tom was going twenty miles east of Mesa on business, and Alice accompanied him. What a sight the country presented! Where men had been planting grain when they passed that way before, a lone horseman's journey on the road a mile south of them could be traced by a cloud of dust that marked his progress and remained in the still, hot air. Not a living thing, bird or beast, could be seen, and a haze of dust was over all.

Everyone slept out of doors on cots [on the hot summer nights]. One night Alice was laying outside, looking up in the cloudless sky, when she heard a roaring sound, like the roar of the river in flood.

"Is that the river?" she asked Tom.

"No. It's the bugs eating the leaves off the cottonwood trees. They've eaten everything else. Haven't you noticed that the birds have left the Valley?"

She hadn't, but then she remembered that she hadn't seen any birds for some time.

[The] report from the cattlemen's committee in California said, "No pasture here. Conditions same as at home." Consternation met this announcement. "Might as well go home and shoot what's left of my cattle to put them out of their misery," said one cattleman as, disconsolately, they separated and went their several ways.

Two of Tom's old friends from the Tonto Country were staying with the Curnows while waiting for this report. When it came, one of them said, "Tom, y'know I just can't go back to see my cattle die, and hanged if I can shoot them. Guess I'll just let them die a natural death all by theirselves."

"Have you lost many?"

"Lost many? Man, I counted seventeen down by the water hole below the corral. They'd tramped all the grass away a long time ago, and [they] just couldn't get back t'the hills. Nothing to eat there either. They ain't a mite of hope. Might as well stay in Phoenix and get a job."

"Nothing was doing there either. Nothing doing any-place if the farms give out, and they'll give out without water."

The three men were on the front porch smoking. They were silent for a few moments, and then Tom asked, "How's the folks up round Tonto?"

"Still getting married. You know Shorty, Tom?"

"No, don't believe I do."

"Sure you do. He's the little feller that fell off'n his horse in the race. Everyone thought he was going to win 'count of his being so small."

"Oh, yes, now I remember him. He was going around with that big woman looked old enough t'be his mother."

"Well, they was married just 'fore I left home. Going to live in her house. She's a widow and pretty well off, if this drought don't take it. Well, sir, she got homelier and homeli-er all the time. You know how her teeth stuck out? Well, they got worse and worse. Bet she could eat the heart out of a pumpkin through a picket fence."

Chapter Nine

The Curnows' house was on a county road, along each side of which a field ditch ran. Cottonwood trees grew along the [ditch bank] edges. The early settlers of Mesa had also outlined each field with trees [so] that their stock would always have shade. Besides, [the trees also] made an excellent windbreak in the sandstorms that often visited that country.

For several days they had watched clouds gather on the peaks, which could be plainly seen from the back of their Mesa home. [The clouds] would grow bigger and bigger until their hearts beat high with hope, only to watch them disappear as night came on. But each day they covered more territory, and each day they stayed longer.

[One night] Alice had lain awake for hours, facing the mountains. Just as she was getting drowsy, she saw through half-closed eyes a flash of heat lightning over Four Peaks. She was wide awake in an instant and sitting on the edge of her cot!

She waited until the flashes were chain lightning and clouds were spreading in all directions. Then, faintly, she heard thunder. Another storm was developing toward [the] McDowell Mountains. Then she called the others; she couldn't wait until morning to spread the good news!

If there was ever a meeting of thanksgiving without words, it was held [that night] in the Curnows' back yard where they watched the storm gathering on various peaks. They knew the country was saved!

The drought was broken and the spirits of the people rose like flowers after a rain. Their greeting was no longer,

"How are you?" But in great excitement they called to one another, "There's water in all the ditches!"

After that drought the people in that part of the country unanimously signed the petition to Congress for a dam on [the] Salt River. The [Roosevelt] dam was begun, which, [in the opinion of G.W.P. Hunt and the citizens of that county], took everything of benefit from Gila County.

⸙

Work piled up in the [blacksmith] shop, which should have made Tom very happy. But almost every night he reported, "Jim had to attend a church meeting again today, was gone from ten o'clock till nearly two."

Murray dropped out of school in the middle of the spring semester, saying that he would never teach and [he] wanted to go to work. Alice pleaded with him to finish, as he was so young and getting along so well, but Murray was determined to go. In his second letter he asked her to send his geometry textbook, that he had decided to come back and finish school.

Alice was delighted! She wrote a cheery little note telling him how glad she was about it, and put the note in his book.

Tom and Alice always provided everything for the children, except spending money for the boys. This they earned, and Murray would have plenty. He didn't return until October, when he had no trouble in keeping up with his class. He was very studious, and [he took] his required reading [home] for Alice to read. One time he brought [Wallace's] *Ben Hur*.

Alice told him she couldn't possibly read it that week because she had to make a number of skirts for young Alice, who was to be in a play dressed in old-fashioned full skirts. While she was clearing the table [to lay out her fabric], Murray followed her about, reading [about] the chariot race after explaining the story to her. After that, Alice read *Ben Hur*.

❦

At that time, about the turn of the century, a great deal was being written in magazines and newspapers about how cheaply one could provide fresh meat for the family. "Just keep a few Belgian hares in your backyard and feed them scraps from your table. It is positively no trick at all."

Tom got directions for building a rabbit house and followed them:

> "Lumber partway up, then screen to the shingled roof. Chicken wire under the dirt floor so the rabbits can't burrow their way out; a walk down the middle of the house with five pens on each side; and always lock your door.

The boys visited the rabbits often, and the family had named all the mothers. A favorite was called "Maggie." The rabbits produced well, and the Curnows had several dinners of young rabbit. One night Murray said, "One of Maggie's rabbits is missing."

"That's impossible," said Tom. "What could happen to it? You've just overlooked it."

But when they investigated, the [rabbit] was gone and the mother was very much excited.

A few days later Alice was passing the [rabbit] house when she heard a commotion. Looking into Maggie's pen, she saw a big bull snake that had swallowed a baby rabbit and couldn't get out. Alice didn't remember what she did, it was so many years later, but she was quite sure that she didn't try to kill the snake. She had never hit anything at which she aimed [except the lizard years ago], and she was quite as frightened as Maggie!

When Tom came home that night the snake was still trying to escape. It was partly out through a small knothole in a board near the bottom of Maggie's pen, but [the lump made by] the baby rabbit was still holding it prisoner. Tom killed the snake, covered the hole with a piece of tin, and they had no more [snake] trouble.

One morning Tom was going to kill a rabbit for dinner. Alice went with him to bring it into the house, as he was in a hurry. He dropped [the dead rabbit] while he was locking the door [to the hutch], and Alice picked it up. In a moment her hands were covered with fleas! She dropped the rabbit and when Tom picked it up his hands were also covered with fleas. Evidently they were leaving the "doomed ship."

Tom turned, opened the door [of the hutch], and drove out all those rabbits, saying, "I wouldn't eat one after seeing those fleas."

Perhaps they stocked that part of the Valley with Belgian hares. That night Alice asked Tom what he was going to do with the rabbit house. He answered, "I thought it would make a good brooder house for incubator chickens. Want to try raising some?"

"Yes, I will."

So their next venture was an incubator [for baby chicks] in their cellar under the house. Alice had very good luck. [She] followed the directions that came with the incubator and soon had more than fifty spring laying hens. She told Tom she would rather rear babies! She could take the babies with her if she wanted to go places, but she had been a prisoner while those chicks hatched and became able to find their own food in the field.

The chicken house was east of the house, halfway across the ranch, so the hens wouldn't be a bother about the house. That fall Alice was very ill, and she required an operation. When she got home [from the hospital], twenty-two of those young hens were gone. Then the incubator came out of the cellar. She would hatch no more chickens.

"Let the hens do their own work," [she declared].

⁕

Next, Tom brought home a gobbler and two hen turkeys, saying, "I have marked them by cutting off their tails [feathers] so we can tell ours from our neighbor's across the road. They will be no trouble to you, as turkeys live on alfalfa."

The next day Alice saw the turkeys occasionally in the field near the house. When Charles came home from school in the late afternoon she told him to look for them, reminding him that theirs had their tails off. Later Charles came in and said, "I went across the road to our neighbors. I'll bet there are two hundred turkeys roosting in the trees over there, and every one has its tail cut off!"

That was their last venture in the turkey raising. Alice asked Tom if they couldn't just live without buying jobs for themselves. He agreed with her, but like most men, as they grow older: They want to live on a ranch or a lot large enough to have things growing, and living creatures about them.

But after the experiences they had just passed through, cows that required no petting from her would be quite enough living things for Alice!

The Curnow ranch was twice as long as it was wide, with a fence across the west end where the house, [a] shed for buggies and tools, and other buildings stood. A fence ran lengthwise in the middle of the field, dividing it into two pastures, with a large trough running [across] the fence so the cows would have fresh water in either field from a windmill tank. There was even an automatic [valve] that closed when the water reached a certain [level] and opened when it fell below a required depth.

The boys milked eleven cows. [They] took the milk in two big cans to a dairy on their way to school, where an

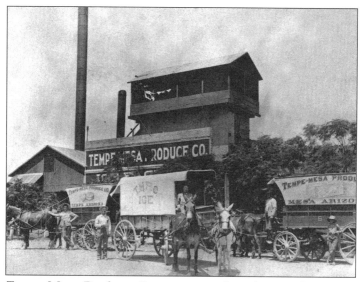

Tempe-Mesa Produce Co. creamery, ice plant and general merchandise, between Mesa and Tempe, Arizona, 1900. *Arizona Historical Society/Tucson, #69655.*

attendant lifted the cans from the wagon, without the boys having to leave their seats. On their return trip from school they picked up the cans. The only farm work Alice had to do then was wash them [for the next day].

Once the alfalfa stand was established, the farmer had only to keep his ditches clean and take the water when it was his turn and time. There was little market for hay, however, since the railroad charged so much for freight that no hay was sold. The milk cows [provided the answer to] this problem. Dairies took care of the milk supply, turning it into butter. Soon a condensed milk factory[7] was established.

[The Valley around Mesa] was a beautiful country of green alfalfa fields as far as one could see. Now that the drought was broken and the dam was being built, the [farmers] worked without dread of another such dry spell. They

7   creamery

planned for a prosper-
ous future and every-
one was happy.

❧

But Tom Curnow
continued to brood over
his partner's church
activities and his neglect
of business. One night
he came home unusual-
ly happy, rubbing his
hands together as he
came in, saying, ""I
found out that Jim is
going to Salt Lake City
to be sealed to his wife
and children [in the
Temple], and I suggest-
ed to him that he buy
me out before going. He
[was] to set the price,
which he did at $150.00.

Alice W. Curnow, c. 1903. *Arizona
Historical Society/Tucson, #8172.*

Not a fourth of the money I have put into the business, but I
said all right. [I was] glad to get out at any price. No more
partners for me."

"But what will you do now, Tom?"

"Don't you worry. I've already bought a [blacksmith]
shop in Tempe."

So in 1902 the Curnows moved to Tempe. Many of
Tom's customers followed him. Business became so good that
he employed four men during the busy summer season. Tom
always kept Alex, a Mexican and an excellent blacksmith,
whom he could trust to do the work if it was necessary for
him to be away for a day.

Tom Curnow and Alex in Tempe Blacksmith shop, c. 1903. *Courtesy Herb and Dorothy McLaughlin Collection, Arizona State University Libraries, MCL 97569.*

Tom paid Alex every Saturday night, when the man promptly got drunk. [He] seldom showed up on Monday morning. About noon one of Alex' little boys would bring a note saying, "My grandmother he die;" then would follow an explanation that he couldn't come to work until after the funeral, about noon. That "Grandmother he died" on an average of three times a month. She was a very convenient relative for Alex to have. Her resurrection, however, was always unannounced.

Again life sailed along tranquilly for the Curnow family. Young Alice and Murray were graduated from Tempe Normal School [then the Teacher's College], in the class of 1903. Alice followed teaching and was principal of one of Globe's schools when she was married to W.C. Holman.

After graduating, Murray took up the study of electricity, in which he had long been interested. Alice tried to dissuade him on account of the danger, but he argued, "Because I know of its danger I shall always be careful."

❧

Just before school began that year Frances became very sick. Doctor Jones diagnosed it as yellow jaundice. Alice wondered why, as she was always very careful of her children's diet. Years later she learned that Frances' brothers would give her money every day to buy ice cream and candy. The Curnows lived across the street from the first store and it was easy for her to get, and she had no appetite for anything else.

Alice thought the heat was the cause of Frances' illness, and she was determined that before the hot weather came the next year she would take her to California. Alice did this, and Frances improved at once. Then Alice was sure that [the] California climate was the cure, not the absence of her brothers.

Tom kept writing for them to come home, but she refused until the hot weather was over. He went to them [in California] in the middle of August for a two-week vacation with her, and they returned September first. It was still above a hundred degrees, but the nights were cooler.

One night Tom said, "Old Man Babbitt (who had bought their ranch on the installment plan) asked me today if he might sell the place to a sheep man. [Babbitt] wants more land to raise wheat and not [to have] so much money in a house. I told him all right, to go ahead."

The money was to be placed in the Kingsbury Bank in Tempe. The Curnows had borrowed the money to build the house from [Elwood C.] Mead, of the Interior Department. Nothing more was said about it until several weeks later, when Mr. Babbitt went to Alice, saying that Tom was too busy to attend to it, and would she find out why he couldn't get the money. He had given possession of the ranch to the sheep man, [but he] couldn't get possession of the forty acres he had bargained for unless he could get the money the sheep man had placed in the Kingsbury Bank for him. Babbitt said, "If I don't get it soon it will be too late to plant grain this year."

Mill Avenue, Tempe, Arizona, 1900. *Sharlot Hall Museum Library/Archives, Prescott, Arizona. (Ci-Tn 216 Pd.)*

"And why can't you get it?"

"That's what I don't know. Can you help me?"

She went with Mr. Babbitt to the bank and asked Mr. Kingsbury why Mr. Babbitt couldn't get his money.

" Because there is no abstract to your property."

"There was an abstract."

"Where is it?"

"I suppose—"

Kingsbury stopped her with, "We don't suppose, in law. Where is it?"

"All right, you have it."

"I have it? I certainly have not."

"Well, as it was turned over to you in the Mead deal I was going to say I supposed you had it, but as in law 'we don't say supposed,' where is it? You don't suppose that Mr. Mead loaned money on a mortgage without an abstract, do you?"

Mr. Kingsbury calmed down and called Mr. Zander of the Phoenix Abstract Company. After Kingsbury [talked with] Mr. Zander, [Zander] asked to speak with Alice.

Tempe and the Salt River from the Butte. *Sharlot Hall Museum Library/Archives, Prescott, Arizona. (Ci-Tn 227P.)*

Alice answered the phone and Mr. Zander said, "Now, Mrs. Curnow, this abstract isn't going to cost you a cent. I will have Mr. Babbitt pay for it."

"No, Mr. Zander, we don't do business that way. The seller provides the deed and abstract to the buyer, and we will give these to Mr. Babbitt."

Turning to Mr. Kingsbury, she said, "You wire Mr. Mead in Cheyenne, at his expense, as he should have returned the abstract, and tell him to provide one at once. And release the money due Mr. Babbitt or he won't have a harvest this year."

"But Mrs. Curnow, if Mr. Babbitt should die on the way home, you will be the loser."

"We will risk that." And Mr. Babbitt got his money. That night she told Tom about it, adding that she thought Kingsbury was dishonest, and [she] would advise him to take their money out of his bank. But Tom said that Kingsbury had been accommodating, and to wait for a while.

Tom Curnow's contemporary [in Tempe] was a Mr. Parry, who had been in business for several years. Like [Tom's ex-partner] Jim, Parry attended meetings and Sunday school while Tom was repairing farm machinery, which was very necessary at that time of year. It pleased the farmers and brought more trade to Tom. Parry's friends resented Tom's success and two of them, young men whose brother ran the biggest saloon in town, were particularly angry about it.

One night, as was his custom, Tom walked down the street to get a cigar. Alice was reading when he returned. She looked up as he very carefully sat down in a chair. She noticed dirt on the sleeve and shoulder of his coat. "Did you fall down?" she asked.

"No. Why?"

"Your coat sleeve and shoulder have dirt on them."

He brushed it off with his hand, saying, "Oh, that."

Tom gave no further explanation, and [he] went to bed at once. The next morning he ate no breakfast. He just drank a cup of coffee and went to the shop. Nor did he eat any dinner. This continued for several days until Alice was very anxious about him.

One morning while dressing Tom looked wildly at Alice and asked, "Who hit me?"

She was terrified, thinking he was losing his mind. She dressed and went to Doctor Jones' office that was just across the street, and told him what she feared. He didn't seem very anxious, but he told Alice to have Tom come to see him at once.

When Tom came back, he told her what had happened.

A gambling game had been running for several days in that big saloon and had become quite exciting. Many of the Normal [School] boys were taking part, and lots of citizens were watching its progress.

Tom joined them, not [as a participant in] the game, but "to see who was ahead," when one of those brothers struck Tom so hard his jaw was broken, so Doctor Jones told him. It was such an unprovoked attack that it ended the game and was the cause of closing the saloon for want of customers.

Alice was glad that their boys were not present at the time [of her conversation with Tom], as their business required their presence in the morning in Phoenix. Those who had been present urged Tom to sue the brothers. But Doctor Jones, who was a friend of both families, settled the trouble by having [them] pay all expenses of having Tom's jaw set by an expert, and for a set of teeth to replace those that had been knocked out. Alice didn't know how Tom endured such suffering without complaint, but he did.

Doctor Jones cared for Tom until his jaw was entirely cured, but he still complained of his stomach. Alice urged him to see Dr. Win Wylie, a noted physician in Phoenix.

The morning he left for Phoenix, Alice was cleaning her kitchen closet. When she was worried she couldn't read or sew; she had to do something physical to take her mind off her troubles. All the pans, pots, and bottles were on the table when Mrs. Heartsfield, a neighbor and a great Women's Christian Temperance Union [WTCU] supporter, came in the back door. She immediately noticed a small flask of brandy that Alice had always kept in the house for that possible rattlesnake bite or the sting of poisonous insects.

"What is that?" she asked.

Alice told her, and Mrs. Heartsfield said, "I'm sorry I didn't know you had it, as I was very sick the other night and would have asked for some."

"I'm sorry, too, for you might have had it. This has been here for I don't know how long."

Mrs. Heartsfield took out the cork, tasted the liquor, and with a disgusted look on her face she said, "Brandy, indeed! It's nothing but cold tea."

When Tom returned and Alice asked if he had been drinking the brandy, he looked guilty, but laughed, saying "It took a WCTU woman to find that out."

"What did Wylie say was wrong with you?" Alice asked him.

"He says that I must stop drinking."

"Drinking! Is that what is the matter with you? And I thought you were cross at times because you were working so hard."

Tom said, "Oh, I don't drink much, but I must not touch it."

The change in Tom was marvelous. He was good-natured and thoughtful. By summer Frances was so well that Alice thought they would remain in Tempe with her husband. He had to stay with his business, which then included the agency for parts [for] farm machinery from Pratt and Gilbert of Phoenix. He also carried his own hardware stock and was quite heavily invested.

Tom hated to live alone, but Frances was overcome by the heat. At the end of the summer he said, "Business, livestock, or not, next year we will go before she suffers so much."

So in 1907 Alice left Tempe on July 3rd, with young Alice and Frances. She wanted Frances to escape the 4th of July heat in Tempe. Tom had to stay behind because he was on a committee for the town celebration.

⁂

July 4, 1907 dawned very hot in Los Angeles. Alice heard someone in the Rosalyn Hotel remark, "It's one hundred three today." They felt the heat much more than in the

Salt River Valley, where the thermometer registered one hundred eighteen for days at a time. (Alice knew this was not the official record, but it was [official] on her thermometer in Tempe, hanging in a shady place.) Arizona's heat is dry, with no prostrations, while in Los Angeles the air was humid.

They remained in the hotel all day on the 4th, but [they] planned to go to Long Beach the next day. Early next morning there was a knock on the door, and Alice opened it to Tom.

"What did you do with the shop?" she asked in amazement.

"I rented it. I would have shut it up otherwise. I'm not going to live alone."

For two weeks they roamed about Los Angeles, went to shows, and thought about going to the Jamestown Fair. But [it was] another humid day that reminded Alice of the summer days in Maine, where they had sunstroke at ninety degrees, and she refused to go.

Tom had to go to San Diego on business, and Alice and the girls went on an excursion to Lake Tahoe. They left the excursion at Truckee, where both Murray and Charlie, who were working in Reno, were waiting for them. They all went to see Alice's parents in Carson City, [Nevada.]

The Curnows had a novel ride on the Virginia and Truckee Railroad, a branch line. Scheduled to leave Reno at two o'clock, the train was backed [up], then went forward, and backed [up] again, then forward again in the railroad yard, until it was 3:00 p.m. when they finally got started. The train stopped frequently, for no apparent reason, until the stops became a joke [among the] passengers. They commented on its stops.

One would say, "The engineer is out there on the flat cutting wood to fire up."

Another stop and, "The engineer dropped his handkerchief."

At one of those stops a woman got on and said something to the conductor, who didn't even wear a uniform. He shook his head and she said, "Well, you *will* stop and pick up my kids."

He asked, "Where do you live?"

Pointing across a wide sand wash to a barn-like building, she said, "Over there."

"Oh, I can't wait till you get them."

"Well, you will stop for my kids, or I'll slap you."

The conductor did stop, and three very dirty little children with a dog got on and greeted the woman with joy.

They were very late getting into Carson City, and Alice wondered if that train would ever reach its Virginia City destination, as it had a stiff climb before it.

Her visit to Carson City made Alice very sad. She remembered when its streets were crowded with people, when the Virginia City mines were furnishing so much silver that the Government built a mint in Carson City to take care of it. Now, the grass was growing between the badly warped boards of the sidewalks, and the streets were never crowded. It reminded her of Goldsmith's *The Deserted Village*.

From her mother's kitchen window Alice could see a few cows wandering about in a pasture that in the 1870s was the picnic grounds. Trainloads of people came from Virginia City to play games and hold contests there. Yes, it made her lonesome [for the past].

Alice's father had an artesian well in his yard. It was not a very extensive well, just a slowly flowing stream of delicious, mountain water, and very cold, as it came from an ordinary water pipe. She asked him why he didn't develop it into a larger stream, and he said, "A man down the street tried to do that and he must have gone through the bedrock, as the water disappeared. Now he has no well. I'm going to let well enough alone."

A large wooden tub caught the water for household purposes, and a bucket hanging on the pipe held water for cooking. A hose was attached to the pipe and [was] moved around the lawn that was always well watered. Tall trees north of the house made a lovely background for the old place.

Alice always found the people of Nevada very friendly and kind, and on the second evening of their stay a busload of young people stopped at their gate. A young lady came in and invited young Alice and Lottie Mullen, who was traveling with them, to join them in a trip to Steamboat Springs, just outside the city, where streams of steam rise from the ground and where a bathhouse was provided.

The girls [accepted the invitation, and] reported spending a very enjoyable evening.

Alice and her family made an interesting [side] trip to the [Nevada] State Prison on a Saturday afternoon when no prisoners were in the yard. Frances had to remain in the office, along with the camera, as on one occasion a prisoner had taken a little child as a shield and escaped.

Years before, when they were excavating for a prison yard, the workers had come upon a cement floor upon which were what appeared to be human footprints coming from the east, made when the cement was soft enough to come up around the foot. Murray, who was six feet tall, couldn't make the stride. Round tracks of an animal accompanied the human ones, and its bones were found in a depression in the cement and placed on a raised bench beside the tracks. Alice had read that Le Conte of the University of California considered the human-like tracks those of a giant sloth.

The cement floor, which the builders had not disturbed on account of its historical value, sloped up to the south wall. Across this floor from east to west and about midway of its length, a wide black line had been painted. A guard on the prison wall shot any prisoner who crossed that line.

It was almost a family reunion on their first Sunday in Carson [City]. Not only all of Alice's children and Lottie Mullen were present, but also her cousin Sam McKenney, with his wife, was there. At dinner young Alice asked her grandfather for some of his reminiscences of early days in California.

"I was eating breakfast in a restaurant in Virginia City when there was a great commotion outside. Nearly everyone left the table and went out. When one returned, I asked what had happened, and he answered, 'Nothing but a man killed. I thought it was a dogfight.'

"A dogfight would have been far more exciting than a man being killed, as there were few dogs but plenty of men. Someone said at the time, 'We had a man killed for breakfast every morning.'"

Alice asked for more, and her grandfather [continued], "Jim Gorman from Whitefield, Maine (Grandfather's birthplace) was with me when I started for California the second time. Everyone carried a carpetbag in those days, but Jim's clothes were sewed up into a perfect ball. He followed me when I went to have my bag checked. When Jim presented his ball, the captain kicked it down into the hold, saying, 'You don't need a check for that. You can claim it anyplace in the world and you will never find another like it.'"

Young Alice said, "Well, go on. That isn't the end of the story, is it?"

"You want the end of it? Well, after crossing the Isthmus of Panama, we were sailing toward San Francisco when we ran into a dreadful thunderstorm. Jim and I were watching it when a flash of lightning cut off a mast and [it] went right through the ship. Water poured through the hole faster than the pumps could pump it out, and the ship was settling when Jim said, 'I have some cheese in the cabin. I've been saving it, but we are going to be drowned. No use wasting it; let's eat it.'

"I agreed with him, and said that I had a bottle of pickles, might as well eat them, too. So we went down but couldn't get in the cabin. It was full of water. Another flash of lightning cut off another mast, turned it over, and plugged up that hole and we were saved."

The boys laughed aloud at their grandfather's story, but young Alice, who was always very dignified, as behooved a schoolteacher, looked at him in utter disdain and asked, "Do you know any more fairy stories, Grandfather?"

"Oh, yes, but this isn't a fairy story. Many years ago I was traveling by stage in the mountains of California, when the driver stopped at a stage barn to add two more horses to our four, as the road ahead was very steep and narrow. I got out to stretch my legs when I saw a twenty-dollar gold piece on the ground at my feet. I picked it up, put it in my pocket, and at the next stop the same thing happened. Another twenty was at my feet. Then I found out it was my own twenty. There was a hole in my pocket."

"No," said Alice, "that wasn't a fairy story. It might happen to anyone."

"Wait," he said. "I haven't finished my story. The road was so steep, narrow, and crooked that sometimes we couldn't see any of the horses except the wheelers. At a sharp turn those wheelers jumped to one side so suddenly that the tongue of the stage was broken off. They continued to jump and plunge because a rattlesnake had jumped at them, but stuck its fangs into the tongue of the stage and couldn't get loose. One of the passengers cut it in two with a scythe and left its head fastened to the tongue."

"Wait a minute, Grandfather, where did the passenger find that scythe?"

"Beside the road, someone had misplaced it. Well, the driver and I went back to a little town we had passed through and [we] got another tongue. When we got back to the stage that tongue with the rattlesnake's head fastened to it had swelled up until it filled the road, and we cut seven cords of wood out of it."

Young Alice didn't ask what they did with the wood, nor why they bothered to cut it, nor did she ask for more stories.

Carson City has a delightful summer climate, and the Curnows had a very pleasant visit. Then the boys returned to work in Reno. About the middle of August young Alice and Lottie left to prepare for their school year. Alice had decided to stay longer with her mother, who was getting quite feeble. Her father was still very active. They were both past seventy-five.

Chapter Ten

A letter came from Tom, [saying] that he had bought four lots in Pacific Beach out near the ocean and would build immediately. Alice knew from experience that he meant *immediately*. "Will have the house ready when you come to San Diego," Tom wrote.

Alice knew just where those lots were, for a real estate man had come to Tempe trying to sell them. But his maps and folders showed them to be nine miles out of San Diego, and Alice wouldn't live that far out. She also knew she would have to work fast to prevent that house building before she had seen the plans. So she [and Frances] packed their satchels and left on the next morning's stage for Lake Tahoe, where she had to go to get their tickets validated.

It was a beautiful trip up the very high mountain that was covered with forest. The road was very steep, and [it] wound back and forth across a ravine. They passed a farm clearing with buildings that, as they climbed higher, looked like dollhouses. From the top of that mountain that in winter would be covered with snow, Alice didn't wonder that Carson City lying at its base could have artesian water.

While they waited at Glenbrook for the boat that would take them across the lake, they visited an old schoolhouse. Its clock had stopped at five o'clock, and an example was still on the blackboard.

At the railroad station Alice checked her bags rather than be bothered with them. Later, while she was getting them in Truckee, Murray, who had come from Reno to see them once more, walked through the entire train looking for them. When his next letter came telling her this, Alice wept a little, thinking of his disappointment and her loss.

She arrived in San Diego in time to stop that house building, for which Tom was later thankful. Landweir, the real estate agent, had told him that the steam train running from San Diego through Pacific Beach to La Jolla was to be electrified immediately, and other improvements were to be installed very soon. He made Tom think that, if he didn't buy at once, he would be losing an opportunity of a lifetime.

Landweir quoted [to them] the money that had been made in buying and selling real estate. He was very convincing, and this was Tom's first experience with real estate agents. After the papers had been signed and the money paid, he laughingly told the Curnows that the seller would get $450.00, "And I will have the rest" of their $1,050.00. Just to show them, she supposed, that money could be made in real estate.

After that they rented a house and waited for those improvements that never came. They paid taxes and for improvements a mile from their property, which [were never made], although their [property] was near the beach. Paving was done a mile away near the hills. (After thirty years of waiting, the taxes got so high that they [finally] let the lots go.)

Nearly every day they saw houses being moved to Pacific Beach, just over the little hill that cut off the ocean breeze, "where you can raise lemons." As if they had not been handed lemons enough! Even the big hotel was moved back from the ocean and [became] part of the Army and Navy school.

People with their savings had come to San Diego, and Landweir-like real estate agents had told them if they would build, the houses would be rented. Many modern houses were built and never occupied. The screens were rotted and hanging from their frames.

Landweir said with a disdainful wave of his hand, "Poor material. Let me order for you and all will be well."

But the Curnows had had quite enough of Mr. Landweir.

⁙

Alice recalled the following summer as one of the happiest of her life. Young Alice came to them [in San Diego] as soon as school closed in Tucson, where she had been teaching. Murray and Charles [arrived] a week later.

Although there were no places of amusement in Pacific Beach, they enjoyed just idling away the time or reading, sometimes having lunch on the beach, or going on picnics on Tom's dray wagon—the latest job he had bought.

On Saturday nights when the train made an extra trip to San Diego, returning at eleven o'clock, young Alice and the boys celebrated by going to a show or [a] dance. They had to be back at the station at eleven, or stay in town that night.

Tom and Murray spent days in the surf, fishing but without any success. Late in the summer Murray caught a fish between four and five inches long. He was delighted! He held it on the line out in front of him toward young Alice, who always had her Kodak near. She took a picture in which the fish looked large enough to provide a good fish story.

The neighbors met with the Curnows once a week, bringing their papers, boxes, and trash to burn on the beach. They told ghost stories, some of which were very shivery and made them think of those long lost at sea. The sea came rolling in on the shore, and with a tired sigh returned to the deep; the phosphorus marked their steps in the moist sand; and a few fleecy clouds floated past the face of the full moon. Yes, it was nice and creepy.

⁙

After the children left, Tom became very restless. There was no business for his dray, as so many people had left their part of the beach to raise lemons. So Tom planted grain for different people on those [not so] valuable lots. After the owners became discouraged and left, then they were anybody's farms.

Alice and Frances continued to go to the beach every day. Frances was getting well and strong. One day they walked about a half-mile up the shore to a large kelp bed, where there were lots of abalone shells. Suddenly Alice noticed that the tide was higher than she had ever seen it. Taking Frances's hand, they ran as fast as they could. The bank was too high and straight to climb, and [in] some places it overhung the beach. By the time they reached a flight of stairs leading from the shore, the water was dashing against the bank.

Alice was terrified, thinking that some catastrophe had happened at sea. She didn't know that the [Pacific] tide that varies very little in summer, sometimes goes as much as seven feet below sea level and more than two feet above in winter.

The grain [was] planted, and again Tom had nothing to do. But he was never discouraged for long. He would try something else. He traded the dray and horse for a year's rent of one of those houses with the screens hanging from their frames. These were repaired, but the house was about half a mile from the railroad, so of course they must have a horse and buggy.

About this time Mr. Nelson, the man who was taking care of their interests in Arizona, wrote that if the Curnows had much cash in Kingsbury's bank, he would advise them to take it out. There was some talk that the bank was in a bad way.

Alice immediately sent a check to her other bank for the balance in the Kingsbury bank. Mr. Kingsbury wrote that he would pay eight percent if they would leave the money with him. The Curnows answered that they didn't consider a bank safe that would pay that much interest, and [they told him] to honor the check.

They were certainly lucky, as a short time after that there was a fire in that bank and the books mysteriously burned, for which Mr. Kingsbury served time in the penitentiary.

For a while Tom was contented. He would take Frances to school, then ride about the beach. But this didn't satisfy him for long. Next he bought a blacksmith shop on a large lot in San Diego, on Third Street near G. One night he laughed, telling Alice, "I always turn my horse loose in that big lot. Today some boys put a pair of large ladies' white drawers, with lace ruffles on the bottoms, on the horse's front legs. They fastened them with a rope around its neck, and put on a sunbonnet with strings tied under its head. [The horse] looked very dejected with its head hanging down, and it received a great deal of attention. "

There was a picture of the horse in the next day's daily paper with the caption, "Humane Man in San Diego." There followed a description of the hot afternoon with no shade for the horse, and how it was dressed to protect it from the flies.[8]

When the year's rent on that house was nearly up, Tom bought a lot in San Diego, on Myrtle Avenue just north of the [Balboa] Park, and adjoining [what was at that time] the Marston property. The lot was fifty feet wide and over one hundred feet long, running down into the bottom of the canyon that passes under the Balboa Bridge. Tom built a very good five-room modern house, but it was the yard that filled him with joy.

After terracing that hill, Tom planted so many trees that Alice wondered if he was planning to go hunting there at

---

8   [*Ed. Unfortunately, a search of newspapers in the San Diego Historical Society Archives did not produce the photo.*]

some future time! (A palm tree in front of the house that was about a foot high at that time was, the last time Alice saw it, towering above the house.)

They had berries and flowers of every description. Tom had wonderful luck. He would drive a crowbar down, set a cutting there, and it grew against all rules or farm directions which said to loosen the surrounding soil.

One night Tom said, "There is no money to be made in a blacksmith shop in San Diego. The biggest store in town sent a little job down, and when I told the man it would be fifty cents, he couldn't order it done until he had reported it to the store. Then another man came to see if he couldn't make a better bargain. That's too cheap for me."

"What will you do with it?" Alice asked.

"I don't know yet."

Sitting down beside him, she said, "I wish you would quit trying to make money here. We have enough from the Arizona property to provide for us, and everything you have tried [in California], you have lost money."

Tom looked at her in astonishment and asked, "And do nothing? I'd rather go fishing again and catch no fish; at least I was trying. Why, I'd go crazy to sit and do nothing. I'll find something yet."

He sold the blacksmith shop, the horse and buggy, and made a payment on a Maxwell car. It had no doors or top, but a nice high windshield, a style that was common at that time. A few days later he phoned Alice to come to the garage where he had bought the car, to ride home with him, as he had learned to drive. She hesitated and asked, "So soon! Are you sure that you can drive safely?"

"Sure I can. I've been driving all morning."

As they came out of that garage, too speedily Alice thought, and turned into D Street—[later] Broadway—a very busy thoroughfare, Alice saw a number of men working on the [street]car track about a block away. There was a pile of dirt on each side of the track, making the road on either side very narrow.

The men were working in a very indifferent manner, as if they didn't get the work done or did was no concern of theirs. One man, who had just emptied a wheelbarrow, was taking plenty of time picking up the handles, when he saw the Curnows coming straight toward him. He showed great speed in climbing that pile of dirt. Shaking his fist at them as they passed, he said "a whole lot of things" that they didn't care to hear! Alice often wondered how Tom missed that wheelbarrow, but he did.

They rode boldly up D Street, crossed Fifth without hitting anything, which [she thought] was miraculous, and [they were] up to Seventh Street when she asked Tom why he didn't slow down. He answered, "I've forgotten how!"

He'd forgotten how? Alice had been frightened before; now she was speechless with fear. Holding her hat firmly, as they seemed to be gaining speed, she saw herself climbing a telegraph pole or landing in someone's cellar, and the coroner being called. Tom, who had been monkeying with the gadgets on that car, must have found the right one, for the car slowed down just before they reached Twelfth Street, where they turned through the park to their home, which they reached in safety.

Tom stopped the car, pushed his hat back on his head, and waited for a moment. Then [he] helped Alice out [of the car] and up the steps, which was necessary.

"Well, that was some ride, wasn't it?"

"It was, and I hope I never have another like it."

"You won't. I know how to stop now."

⚜

While Alice was preparing dinner one day Tom brought home a magazine and read an ad of how much money could be made in raising mushrooms in your cellar or barn. [There were] directions on how to build an especially constructed house for them:

> Double plank walls with space between, filled with dirt; plank roof with thick covering of earth; door of same design; ventilator of box about eight inches square extending through and above the roof two or three feet, and cover the ventilator very carefully with fly screen.

Then followed directions for preparing the mushroom beds on each side of [a] center walk through the house "that the mushrooms can be picked without stepping on the beds."

"It reminds me of the rabbit house you built long ago. Why, do you suppose, are you to cover that ventilator with screen? To keep out the bull snakes?"

Tom didn't answer her, but [he] built that mushroom house and the mushrooms came up just as predicted. They had delicious dinners and sold all Tom could grow, with orders to bring more.

Then one morning Alice saw him shoveling the mushroom beds down into the canyon, [muttering], "They are alive with fly blows."

So that was why the screens were ordered! Alice wondered what Tom would do next.

Tom had become acquainted with some of the councilmen, and with his car, he was given work in the Sanitary Department of the City [of San Diego]. In this work he became familiar with the construction business, and [he] decided that would be his next venture.

He would pay cash for a lot and mortgage it to the bank for enough money to build a house, which could then be sold more readily on monthly payments. [He would sell the house] with a down payment of the price of the lot, and turn the agreement over to the bank that was glad to have that business.

Tom allowed himself five dollars a day, with a bonus for the building, according to its price. He had good workmen and had at last evidently found his niche.

❧

A letter from Murray dated Los Angeles read, "I will be with you to spend Christmas, and [I] will not come alone."

Alice felt sure that he was bringing his wife, although she didn't know that he was engaged. She was right. They visited with Tom and Alice for a few weeks, and then Murray [went] back to Arizona to work at his trade.

Again, Alice tried to comfort herself with Murray's promise to be careful. As he had been working in electricity for nearly eight years, she felt assured that he would exercise caution.

❧

Frances had been studying the piano for two years. She was attending the Florence Heights School and [she] was always urging Alice to come to their entertainments, where she would hear Freddie Olson play on the violin. Alice promised that sometime she would go.

One day Frances was so insistent that Alice promised to attend. Unfortunately, she called for a friend who was also going, one who was always late. No matter what time was set, Alice had to wait for her. That day was no exception. When they arrived, Freddie had [already] played his solo. Frances was so disappointed that she couldn't keep the tears back.

Alice knew at once why her daughter had wanted her to hear Freddie, and she asked Frances if she would like a violin. Frances said, "Could I have one?"

From school that day they went to the San Diego Institute of Music, where Chesley Mills taught violin. Frances had her first lesson, which was how to hold the violin and bow and, most important for a beginner, how to stand. [She was] to practice before a mirror to gain this position.

Tom and Frances did excellent work in their different [endeavors]. Frances was majoring in music in high school, and Tom was selling houses just as fast as they were built.

❧

Murray had sent for a set of his books on electricity, which Alice thought was of eight volumes, for his helper, whom he was going to teach. Being in a hurry, Tom boxed them at once and Alice didn't write her usual note to enclose.

October 11, 1911, was a lovely day in San Diego. The sky was clear and the air was sharply cold. It was a day that made one glad to be alive. Alice had been sewing when the phone rang. The operator was very careful that she had the right number.

"Is this the T.W. Curnow residence?" she asked.

Alice answered, "This is Mrs. T.W. Curnow speaking, and I will take the message."

"Have you family in Miami [Arizona]?"

"Yes, our son lives there." Alice was happy; thinking that Murray was coming home for the holidays, as the children did every year.

The operator said, "Then listen carefully. The message says, 'Murray received an electric shock and died at eleven thirty. Signed, Charlie.'"

Alice had no idea what she did for some time. Then she noticed she hadn't hung up the receiver, nor had she called Tom. She called, and he came to her at once. A blow like that was indescribable; she did not try to express it.

The Curnows left San Diego for Globe on the first train that afternoon. All that night and the next day Alice was between hope and despair: One moment she hoped that Murray might be revived; the next, she [thought] Charles wouldn't send that message if there was any hope.

When they reached Bowie they tried to phone, but the wires were down due to a recent heavy storm. Alice asked an electrician what effect electricity had on the human body, and he answered, "It cooks the blood."

Then she knew there was no hope.

After the funeral, [Murray's] wife told Alice that the set of books had come the night before his death, and he had turned every leaf of every book, looking for a note from her. That added to her sorrow, to think that she had failed him.

Tom and Alice returned to San Diego, where Frances was left with a neighbor, and took up their lives again. It would never be quite the same with Murray gone.

⁘

A letter from Charles said, "I am sending a picture of the reason I am not coming to see you this summer. Meet Miss Etta Kieren, whom you will see about Christmas time as Mrs. Charles Curnow." He tried to describe a very pretty girl in the picture, standing among beautiful trees in Wheatfields [Arizona].

⁘

Tom had done so well in building that he branched out and had four houses under construction, each carrying a mortgage. When the World War [I] came on, all construction ceased. Nothing could be sold and everything was given over to preparation for war.

He had sold all their property in Arizona to invest in San Diego. Frances had one more year in the San Diego Conservatory of Music, of which Chesley Mills was now the head, before she would be graduated as a teacher of violin.

Tom came in one day and asked, "Do you know we have but two hundred dollars in the bank? I am going back to Arizona to see what I can find there. I feel more at home there than anyplace else in the world."

Alice wondered what Tom could possibly do there, as he was sixty years old and all his old friends were gone. But Tom did look around and found that auto stages were carrying

Thomas W. Curnow, c. 1924. *Arizona Historical Society/Tucson, #8171.*

passengers from Miami to Globe, about nine miles, for thirty-five cents each way, as quickly as they could be loaded. The railroad charged fifty cents each way, with but two trains a day.

The autos were a great convenience, and [they] prospered. But they were not organized. Each driver tried to make a quick run. They passed each other on curves and hills, and raced with no regard for the safety of their passengers. There were no stations and no time schedule.

Tom, with eleven other men, incorporated [the Lower Miami Stage Company in 1916] and ran autos on scheduled times to Lower Miami [and Claypool] for ten cents, while another company took the Globe run. Tom had such good credit through his building [activities that] he was able to buy a big car on time, and to take it out of the State of California. In this new venture Tom was again successful. He made enough to save what he had invested in San Diego.

The following year [1917] Frances graduated from the San Diego Conservatory of Music as a violin teacher and an orchestra leader, without having missed a lesson. But there were so many excellent musicians in [the San Diego area that] she decided to return to Globe with her sister Alice, who with her little son had been spending the summer with her parents. Frances found pupils in Globe and was very successful.

Alice remained in California for another year, until their houses were either sold or rented. When she returned to Arizona [in 1918], the Salt River Valley that was so successful when they left in 1907 was a picture of ruin. [*Ed. She explains why:*]

Several years before the Curnows had lived there, the Government had established an experimental station several miles south of Tempe. It was of great benefit to the farmers in that region. They could get any information they wanted concerning agriculture. The orange scale disease, for instance, had been imported to Arizona to discover what would kill it. It died without treatment, so Alice was told,

Keystone Avenue, Miami, Arizona, 1920s. *Arizona Historical Society/Tucson, #56897.*

perhaps on account of the hot, dry climate. Cantaloupes grew abundantly and competed with those of Rocky Ford. Excellent grapes were also grown there.

Then it was reported that [long staple] cotton could be profitably grown in the Valley. Several farmers sold their milk cows, dug up their alfalfa, and planted cotton. For a few years this was very profitable; more and more farmers followed their neighbors' example, until not a quart of milk could be purchased that was produced in the Valley. All milk was imported; the condensed milk factory closed.

Like the tulip growers of Holland, people went crazy over cotton. Then [in 1920] the crash came. Prices went down and there was no [market] for cotton that was stored in warehouses in Phoenix or on the ranches. Still people planted cotton, until they could no longer get credit.

A neighbor of the Curnows in Miami told them that he had a large general store in Glendale, north[west] of Phoenix, and that he had to close, as he couldn't get or give credit. [Consequently], he was working in the mine at Miami [Arizona]. An old friend [of Alice] whose husband [had] died, rented her ranch near Mesa and went to Globe to live with her daughter. [Her friend returned] to the Valley to learn why she was getting no rent. On her return, she told Alice that conditions were so bad there that she didn't even ask for the rent.

[Finally] the merchants and bankers of the [Salt River] Valley held a meeting and decided to extend credit to the farmers. Alice didn't know what the conditions [of the loans] were; perhaps the farmers were to plant no more cotton.

⚜

Tom Curnow took the early morning stage run to take men to the station, where they met the train to the Inspiration Mine. The younger men didn't want [this run], as they had to rise so early. This run was very profitable, but because Tom's eyes were failing he never drove after dark. He had his glasses changed frequently. Alice thought nothing of this; just that old age was coming on. And she had never been associated with anyone who was blind.

Frances was married to John Griffin in April 1920. In September of that year Tom said, "I have rented the car and stock. [I] think it will help my eyes if I rest them for awhile."

Alice was still blissfully ignorant of the tragedy they were approaching. Tom was so patient and uncomplaining! About that time he went to Phoenix to consult a doctor who was highly recommended. He changed Tom's glasses too frequently, Alice thought, so she went [to an appointment] with him. At last she had become anxious.

The doctor again advised [a] change of glasses. Alice followed him into another office, where he told her that if Tom were not operated on immediately he would go blind. "Why didn't you tell him before?" she asked.

"I didn't want to worry him. I will perform the operation for five hundred dollars."

Alice gave him no answer. They returned to Miami that afternoon and left for Los Angeles the next morning, where they went to a private hospital that was highly recommended, and an operation was performed on Tom's eyes.

The doctor told them a cataract was forming. They were to return when Tom couldn't see the sun between his open fingers; the cataract could easily be removed when it had developed to the right stage. For some reason Alice had no confidence in that doctor. Tom had. The Curnows returned to Miami and he faithfully looked through his fingers every morning.

When Tom could no longer see the sun, they returned to Los Angeles. Alice insisted that they go first to Dr. McCoy, of whom they had heard great things. After a brief examination he asked Tom if he suffered much pain.

Tom answered, "Not at all."

Dr. McCoy turned to Alice and gruffly said, "This man is blind. It's too late to try to help him now. Why didn't you come before? He has no cataract."

His diagnosis was hardening of the arteries in the eye, and the doctor wondered that Tom hadn't suffered [more]. Alice told the doctor [of] the treatment Tom had received; he made no comment.

It was a terrible blow to Alice, and she cried bitterly for a few minutes before they left the doctor's office. From there they went to Dr. A. Ray Irvine, who offered the same opinion, but more kindly. Alice couldn't give up. She pleaded with Tom to let her take him to the Mayo Clinic for further examination. He was sure the doctors were right, there was no help for him, and he refused to go to Mayo's, or to try anyone else.

⚜

When Alice came from the market one day [in 1930], Tom was sitting on the couch in front of the three big windows on the west end of their living room, looking very dejected. She sat down beside him. Putting her arm across his shoulders, she said, "My, but it's nice and cool in here! It's terribly hot outside. Aren't you glad you don't have to go out?"

Tom took her hand in one of his and, patting it with the other, he said, "Do you know, I would like to go to that hospital just to hear what that doctor would have to say."

"All right, I'll make an appointment for tomorrow."

The next day at the hospital the doctor gave Tom an examination. Alice didn't remember what his report was, because Tom was suffering terribly. Alice called Dr. Irvine and he prescribed [medication] for Tom, and advised having the affected eye taken out.

Tom agreed, as he said he couldn't stand the pain. Dr. Irvine made all arrangements, telling Alice to take Tom to the hospital at once.

After another examination the doctor said, "I still advise taking out that eye."

This was done, and Alice visited Tom every day. He was so lonesome. He had been there several days, when one day as she entered the room a nurse was working over him. Alice asked, "Is he worse?"

The nurse answered, "No, but he thought that he could go to the bathroom without calling a nurse, and he fell in the tub."

Tom said that he wasn't hurt, but Alice stayed with him longer than usual that day. She read papers and letters and told him all the news.

Another day when she arrived he was laughing. He told her, "The nurses here are so kind. One of them came in this morning saying, 'Dad, I've come to give you an alcohol rub.' I said, 'All right.'

"After a while another nurse came and said, 'Dad, I've come to give you an alcohol rub.' Again I said, 'All right, go ahead,' but when another nurse said that she had come to give me an alcohol rub I said, 'All right, but I've had two this morning.' She laughed and said she thought I had had enough."

Tom got along very well, and when the doctor said he might go home, Alice took him first to a barbershop for a shave. He had always shaved himself, and, if she didn't move his things, he required no help in dressing.

That morning after coming home he felt of his face, saying, "That wasn't a very good shave," and he shaved again.

What surprised him was that Alice's housekeeping took so much time. He was waiting for her to read the daily papers to him. Besides the morning and evening daily Los Angeles papers, they got their home paper. This was Tom's only interest. He would ask, "What are you doing now?"

"Just washed the dishes, and cleaned the kitchen,

prepared vegetables for dinner, washed a few socks for you. Now I will make the bed and clean up the bedroom."

"Then will you be through?"

"No, time to get dinner then."

It was quite heartbreaking to see Tom feeling his way along the wall. He had been so active. When they went out he always used a cane, and she took his arm.

The Curnows passed the pleasant autumn days comfortably. Tom was a very light eater, but he must have his three meals a day. On November 11, 1930, they had dinner as usual. Alice had cleared up the kitchen and had just read the evening paper to Tom, when he jumped to his feet. Catching his throat with his hand he said, "I have a terrible pain."

Alice rushed to him, saying, "I'll call the doctor."

"No, I want no more doctors."

He undressed as usual and got into bed, saying, "My hands are terribly cold."

Alice had very little hot water, but [she] put what she had in the hot water bag and, after rubbing Tom's hands, [she] put the hot water on them.

He said, "That's better now."

Alice turned toward the kitchen to get more hot water, but Tom called her before she had crossed the hall. When she went back to him he was gone.

Someone called his physician, but he was out on a sick call. The emergency hospital was called.

Alice was kneeling beside Tom when the doctor and several officers came. The doctor pronounced Tom dead just as Frances entered the room. With the tears streaming down her face, she asked, "What happened to him, Mother?"

Alice told her. She didn't know who led her from the room. Tom's dying without a doctor [present] required a post mortem, which disclosed heart failure due to hardening of the arteries.

Charles came from Miami [Arizona] and Alice came from Douglas to be with their mother. Tom was buried in Forest Lawn Cemetery [in Glendale, California].

Alice missed her husband greatly. He had been at home so much during the past ten years that it was hard [for her] to become accustomed to living alone. They had celebrated their fiftieth wedding anniversary on December 18, 1929, and December 18, 1930, was an especially lonesome day for her.

Frances made the holidays pass pleasantly, as she always did, and looking over her manuscript gave Alice something to do, which was a blessing. After a busy life of rearing four children, then having Tom to care for in his helpless condition, to find herself with nothing to do would have been too much of a sudden change for a contented old age.

"So, if this is never published, it will have served a purpose."

⚜

Alice had spent more than a year with Charles and Etta in Arizona when Frances wrote that she was going to Los Angeles for a vacation from Seattle, where her husband had been transferred. [She urged Alice] to join her there, since she had found the summers in Arizona very trying after her sojourn in Los Angeles.

Young Alice and her son John and daughter Joan met Alice at the train. She was shocked at her [eldest daughter's] changed appearance. She had been to Mayo's for an operation for cancer, and after several visits there for a check-up, the doctors pronounced her cured. But when Alice saw her, she knew she was doomed. She remained with her until her death on December 30, 1934. At that time her husband was in Central America, and [so] Alice stayed with her grandchildren until his return.

[*Ed. Mrs. Curnow's manuscript concludes:*]

As this covers the high spots in my life, there is not

much more to write, except that I am thankful that I still have a son and daughter left to me, who both visit me at least once a year. I find the climate of Los Angeles very pleasant.

⚜

[*Ed. Alice J. Curnow passed away October 27, 1940, in Los Angeles, California. She was laid to rest beside her husband at Forest Lawn Cemetery.* The Journey with Tom *was complete.*]

Appendix I

Chronology of the Curnow Family

1855   Tom Curnow born "somewhere in Michigan"- February 11

1861   Alice Jane Donovan born in North Whitefield, Maine - February 13

1872   Tom Curnow moves to Virginia City, Nevada

1877   Donovan family moves to Gold Hill, Nevada

1879   Tom and Alice marry in Gold Hill, Nevada - December 18

1881   Tom arrives in Globe City - January 6

1881   Alice arrives in Richmond Basin - March 17

1881   Tom and Alice establish home in Richmond Basin

1882   Alice born in Gold Hill, Nevada - February 14

1882   Alice and baby return to Richmond Basin - April

1882   Tom and Alice move to Globe - November

1883   Curnow and Scholefield purchase lot and saloon building in Globe

1884   Murray born in Globe - November 4

1885   Tom and Alice move to farm downriver from Dudleyville, back to Globe

1885   Mine closes in Globe, reopens

1886   Charles born in Globe

1887   Curnows move to Pioneer, back to Globe

1887   Mine closes again

1888   Alice and children visit Gold Hill

1888   Tom opens meat market, Curnow & Co., in Globe

1888   Tom opens carpenter shop in Globe

1889   Charles and Mary Starr move to Mesa

1891   Severe flood in Arizona

1891   Helen born in Globe - December 23

1892   Alice and children spend summer in Mesa with Mary Starr

1893   Lavina "Bean" Walker married

1894   Tom elected delegate to convention at Republican primary - September

1895   Curnow & Middleton advertisement appears in Globe newspaper

1895   Helen dies of diphtheria in Globe - December 17 - age 4

1896   Alice and children move to Mesa in February, return in August

1897   Tom goes to work for Silver Reef Company below Casa Grande - April

1898   Frances born in Globe - July 17

1898   Tom purchases blacksmith business, residence and 20 acres of land in Mesa

1898   Curnows move to Mesa

1902   Curnows move to Tempe, Tom opens blacksmith shop at 6th Street and Mill

1903   Alice and Murray graduate from Tempe Normal

1903   Alice marries W.C. Holman in Douglas; children John and Joan

1907   Curnows move to Los Angeles in July, then San Diego

1907   Alice and girls meet boys in Reno, visit her parents in Gold Hill

1907   Charles marries Etta Kieren

1907–1918   Curnows own home on Myrtle Avenue in San Diego

1910   Murray marries.

1911   Murray electrocuted at Miami Copper Company - October 11

1913   Alice is principal of Noftger Hill School in Globe

1916 Frances graduates from San Diego Conservatory of Music, starts teaching music in Globe

1916 Curnows move to Miami

1917 Curnow becomes partner in Lower Miami Stage Company, serves on Sanitation Committee

1920 Frances marries John Griffin - April

1920 Tom and Alice return to Los Angeles

1923 Tom and Alice living in Miami; Charles owns Unique Restaurant

1925 Alice elected corresponding secretary of Miami Women's Club - April

1929 Tom and Alice celebrate 50th wedding anniversary - December 18

1930 Tom dies in Los Angeles - November 11 - age 76

1934 Alice Curnow Holman dies of cancer in Los Angeles - age 52

1940 Charles on Gila County Board of Supervisors

1940 Alice dies in Los Angeles - October 27 - age 79

Appendix II

Newspaper Clippings

Paper Trail of the Curnow Family

(Globe) *Arizona Silver Belt*

05/06/1885
Thomas Curnow was here for several days this week and disposed of his cattle. It is his intention to start a hog ranch near Riverside, where he has 160 acres of fine land under fence. [*Ed. Alice didn't mention the hog ranch.*]

10/13/1888
Tom Curnow has opened a carpenter shop in the Anderson Building, corner of Broad and Oak streets. He is expecting his wife and children home in a few days from Gold Hill, Nevada, where they have been spending the summer with relatives.

02/02/1889
Mr. and Mrs. Charles Starr arrived from Florence on Tuesday, to remain several days, and are the guests of Mr. and Mrs. Thos. Curnow. They are preparing to soon take up their permanent abode at Mesa City, Maricopa County, where Mr. Starr has purchased a farm and will remove his cattle.

06/18/1892
Mrs. T.W. Curnow and children left Thursday morning

to spend the summer with Mrs. Chas. H. Starr at Mesa. Mr. Starr, who was here on business for a few days, accompanied them.

09/29/1894

At the Republican primary, Globe precinct, held in the Court House last Saturday, the following delegates to the county Convention, Oct. 2nd, were elected: . . . Thos. W. Curnow . . . .

06/22/1895

Thos. S. Curnow, Jas. Anderson, Lee Middleton and Shirley Neff left last Sunday, horseback, for Salt River Valley. Mr. Curnow will visit Charles Starr and family at Mesa, and the others will most likely continue on to Phoenix, thence to Prescott where they will celebrate the fourth.

07/06/1895

Thos. S. Curnow returned from a visit to Phoenix and Salt River Valley. Mr. Curnow spent some time with Mr. and Mrs. Chas. Starr, who have one of the prettiest places in Mesa. Mr. Curnow also owns a tract of fine land near Mesa, which he will have set out with almond trees. He is enthusiastic in his praise of Salt River Valley.

10/19/1895

The advertisement of Curnow & Middleton, blacksmiths and wagonmakers, appears in this issue of the BELT. The members of the firm are too well known to require any introduction from us. Mr. Lee Middleton gives his personal attention to the business, and has a most competent assistant in W.A. Buel, an expert woodworker. We confidently recommend the firm as worthy of patronage.

Advertisement:

12/14/1895

Mr. and Mrs. Charles H. Starr, of Mesa, arrived on Thursday, having come via Silver King and the trail. Mrs. Starr will remain to take care of her sister, Mrs. Curnow and her children, sick with diphtheria, but who are, happily, convalescing. Mr. Starr will return home today.

12/21/1895

Helen Curnow, youngest child of Mr. and Mrs. Thomas W. Curnow, died on Tuesday last of diphtheria. The little one was apparently improving, but as is often the case in that [illegible] and dread disease, there was a sudden change for the worse and death came suddenly to the little sufferer. Mrs.

Curnow and her three remaining children are reported to be convalescent. Friends of the family, while unable to render assistance, sympathize deeply with them in their grief.

02/20/1896

Mrs. Charles [sic] Curnow arrived from Globe Tuesday with her little daughter, Alice, and son, Master Charles, and is visiting her sister, Mrs. Charles Starr.—*Mesa Free Press.*

06/11/1896

Thomas S. Curnow leaves for Mesa today to visit his family for two or three weeks.

07/02/1896

Tom Curnow is back from Mesa, where he enjoyed a visit with his family.

08/06/1896

Mrs. T.S. Curnow and children, who have been in Mesa for several months, returned home last Thursday. The late flood so endangered their pretty home on north Broad Street that Mr. Curnow reluctantly moved the house to a more desirable location at the east end of town, where the family now resides.

01/07/1897

Mrs. Chas. H. Starr arrived from Mesa last week for a short stay, accompanied by her niece, Miss Alice Curnow, who has been visiting Mrs. Starr and family for some time. . . .

04/08/1897

T.S. Curnow left on Monday for the mines of the Silver Reef Company, below Casa Grande, of which J.H. Canavan is superintendent. Mr. Curnow has been engaged as master mechanic for the company at a good salary. Mrs. Curnow and children will remain in Globe for the present.

11/18/1897

Thos. W. Curnow returned home on a visit last Friday from the Peck mines, fourteen miles south-west of Casa Grande, where he has been for the past eight months, filling the position of master mechanic for the company. The claims owned by the company comprise two groups, copper and silver, and which Mr.Curnow believes are valuable properties. The company will probably erect lixiviation works for reduction of the ores. The principal stockholders are prominent St. Louis men with ample capital. John H. Canavan, formerly with the Old Dominion Copper Company, is superintendent.

02/03/1898

Thos. W. Curnow returned last Thursday from Salt River Valley, Maricopa County. Mr. Curnow informs us that he has bought into the best blacksmithing business in Mesa, and with his family will remove there about the 15th inst. Mr. Curnow owns the handsome residence in Mesa, erected by the late Dr. Alex Trippel and also a tract of 20 acres of fine land on the outskirts of town. He has sold the family home in Globe to James Richards.

The Daily Globe (**Arizona**)
10/12/1911

Killed by Electric Shock * * * Murray Curnow Meets With Sudden Violent Death at Miami Copper Plant * * * Was Warned Not to Begin Before Noon * * * A Sister, Miss Alice Curnow, Was Attending Teachers' Institute at Thatcher

Murray Curnow, an electrician in the employ of the Miami Copper Company, met sudden and violent death yesterday forenoon by electrocution. Curnow was disconnecting

the wires from a switchboard in the elevator shaft of the
Miami Mill Sampling Works when he was killed.

He had been assigned to the work of disconnecting the
wiring of a motor and switchboard, for the object of replacing
the motor by a smaller one; but when Chief electrician Scott
told him to do the work he warned Curnow not to begin the
task until after 12 o'clock, when the current would be cut off
during the noon hour. Curnow, however, decided to begin
the work sooner than he was told and entered the shaft at
about 11 o'clock. He disconnected two wires from the
switchboard and "tapped" the exposed ends.

At this time his helper left him for other tools and when
he returned two or three minutes later, Curnow was writhing
in his death agony. His body was wedged in between the
switchboard and a metal stairway so tightly that three men
had to exert their strength to extricate his body. From the
position of the body when found and the burns upon his
body it is supposed that he met his death as the result of two
shocks, the first not fatal. The concrete floor upon which he
stood is not wholly non-conductive because of the presence
of the steel rods used for reinforcement, and probably he
received a shock through the pliers with which he was disconnecting the wires that, while not severe, was still strong
enough to throw him against the steel banister of the stairway, thus making a complete circuit though his body and
causing almost instant death. Upon the index finger of his left
hand there is a deep burn where the current entered from the
pliers he was using to cut the wires. Upon the elbow of the
right arm there is another but less severe burn. It is thought
that the latter marks the point of his body that first touched
the steel stairway, thus completing the circuit of the current
through his body. The body also shows slight abrasions,
apparently caused by contact with the steel railing as he fell.
They are on the upper side of the left wrist, his breast and the

right side of the face. When found by his assistant the pliers had dropped from Curnow's hand and were lying near him on the floor.

Curnow is a native of Globe, having been born in this city 27 years ago. His parents reside in San Diego, Cal.; his brother, Charles Curnow, and Miss Alice Curnow, his sister being residents of Globe. Mrs. Charles Starr, a resident of Globe, is also a sister [*sic*] of the dead man. He leaves a wife, having been married about eleven months. Charles Curnow went to Miami immediately upon the sad news of his brother's death and returned with the body to Globe after the coroner's jury had rendered its verdict. Yesterday evening Miss Alice Curnow returned from Thatcher, having been summoned by wire. She is a schoolteacher in the Globe public schools and had been attending the Teachers' Institute in the valley town.

Upon being apprised of the death of Curnow, Coroner Lafayette F. Nash summoned J.S. Miles, Parker Medlin, Eugene Jones, Burt Welch, J.H. Fitzpatrick and T.R. Gee as a coroner's jury and an inquest was held upon the body at the scene of the tragedy. The verdict of the jury is as follows:

"We, the undersigned, impaneled as a coroner's jury to inquire into the death of E.M. Curnow, do find that he was employed as an electrician by the Miami Copper company, and that he came to his death about 11 o'clock on October 11, 1911, by coming in contact with a live wire while engaged in the discharge of his duties; and we further find that no one was responsible for his death; and we further find that the Miami Copper company is in no way responsible for his death, as he had been instructed to do this work after 12 o'clock when all power would have been shut off."

Curnow was a popular young fellow whose loss will be mourned by many besides the members of his own family. His death is a distinct loss to the community, for he was an industrious and manly citizen. His body rests in the chapel of Jones & Son. Preparations for interment have not yet been made.

10/13/1911

Await Curnow's Father.

The body of Murray Curnow, who was electrocuted at the plant of the Miami Copper company Wednesday, is at the chapel of F.L. Jones & Son, where it will be held pending the arrival of his father, who has wired that he had left San Diego Wednesday night for Globe. Upon Mr. Curnow's arrival arrangements for the funeral services will be made. Miss Alice Curnow, who was attending the teacher's institute at Thatcher, has returned to Globe.

10/15/1911

The Funeral of E.M. Curnow Today

The funeral of Edward Murray Curnow will be held from the Baptist church this afternoon at 2 o'clock. The services will be conducted by the Rev. J.M. Barnhart and the Interment will be in the general cemetery.

Mr. and Mrs. Thomas Curnow of San Diego arrived in Globe last night for the purpose of attending the funeral.

10/16/1911

Murray Curnow's Funeral Held Yesterday * * * Attended by Host of Friends and Relatives of the Departed * * * Was Native of Globe * * * Death was Caused by Electrocution at Miami Last Wednesday

The funeral of Murray Curnow, the young electrician

whose tragic death by electrocution occurred at Miami last Wednesday, occurred here yesterday afternoon and was attended by a host of friends of the departed man and bereaved family. The last rites were held at the Methodist [*sic*] church, the sermon being delivered by Rev. John M. Barnhart.

Murray Curnow was a native of Globe, having been born in this city in 1884. He was an exceptionally well-liked young man, competent, clean living and industrious, and his sudden and tragic death is regretted by hundreds besides his bereaved wife and relatives.

His parents arrived here from their home in San Diego, Cal., to be at the funeral of their son, and his brother, Charles Curnow, his sister, Miss Alice Curnow, and his widow, were together in their bereavement. He had been married less than a year.

The funeral of the lamented man was one of the largest ever seen in Globe, eloquent testimony of the high regard in which Murray Curnow was held by the people of Globe.

Miami (*Arizona Silver Belt*)
11/12/1930

"Dad" Curnow Passes Away in L.A. While Peacefully Asleep * * * One of Arizona's Best-Known Pioneers Goes to Great Beyond in Full Health During Slumber at Night * * * T.W. Curnow, affectionately known throughout the Miami-Globe district as "Dad" Curnow, and one of the pioneer residents of Arizona, died last evening at his home in Los Angeles, to which he had moved about a year ago.

In Good Health "Dad" Curnow's death came quietly without warning. He had not been ill. Last evening he went to bed and died during sleep. He leaves a widow, Mrs. T.W. Curnow and a daughter, Mrs. John Griffith, of Los Angeles, a son Charles Curnow of Miami and a daughter, Mrs. W.C. Holman of Douglas.

Mr. Curnow came to Globe in 1881. He was 76 years old. He was born 'somewhere in northern Michigan' in 1855. Soon afterwards his parents removed to Connecticut.

In 1872, at the age of 17 years, he was engaged in carrying silver bullion from the famous Comstock mines at Virginia City, Nev., to the United States mint at Carson City. One of his clients was the then governor of the state. This little item alone identifies "Dad" Curnow as one who was imbued with the pioneering spirit, which settled the west.

At Carson City, "Dad" had the excellent good fortune to win the heart and hand of the present Mrs. T.W. Curnow. They were married there in 1879.

In Globe, 1881. With the waning of the boom silver mines of Nevada, "Dad," turned his attention to the new silver discoveries of Arizona. The Curnows arrived in Globe in 1881. His first employment was as a butcher, a trade he had learned in his early youth.

Then followed employment in the bonanza silver district of Richmond Basin north of Globe, as blacksmith and tool dresser, another of his trades.

In 1883 he became head blacksmith for the Old Dominion mines and held the job nine years. Then he filled the position of master mechanic at the same mines for another seven years.

Following which the Curnows moved to the Salt River Valley where they engaged in farming. But "Dad" was an expert blacksmith and mechanic, and incidentally, had learned the carpenter trade somewhere along the line. So it was inevitable that he should open up general repair shops at Tempe and Mesa.

Then the Curnows, having prospered, moved to San Diego, where "Dad" was employed in the sanitary department of that city for three years. It was there he established an enthusiasm for the study of municipal sanitation, which has grown rather than diminished with the encroaching years.

In Miami. In 1916, the Curnows came to Miami. Mr. Curnow engaged in the stage business between Miami and Claypool. For five years he was president of the company.

In 1924 he was elected to the town council and was for several terms chairman of the committee on sanitation.

Funeral services will be held in Los Angeles, details to be announced later.

(Tucson) *Arizona Daily Star*
n.d.

"Arizona Pioneer Depicted in Book"

The life of a pioneer Arizona woman is told in the story, "The Journey with Tom," which was presented this week in manuscript form to the Arizona Pioneers' Historical society. Mrs. T.W. Curnow of Los Angeles made the gift and is the author of her own story. She came to Arizona in 1881 and with her husband, Tom, went by stage from Casa Grande to Globe where she lived for many years. The document tells all her early day experiences.

Phoenix **(Arizona)** *Gazette*
10/10/1940
Dateline Globe – Special to the *Gazette*

"Death Takes Alice Curnow"

Mrs. Alice Curnow, who came to Arizona more than sixty years ago, died at her home in Los Angeles some time during the night Saturday, according to word received by relatives here.

About eighty-three years old, she had apparently been

in normal condition when she retired Saturday night. When relatives went to awaken her Sunday morning they found her dead.

Charles Curnow, member and former chairman of the Gila county Board of Supervisor, was hunting in the Sierra Ancha when notified of his mother's death. A daughter, Mrs. John Griffin, lives in Kansas.

Mrs. Curnow left Miami, where she had lived for many years after moving there from Globe, in 1934.

Bibliography

Books and Journal Articles

Arizona Business Directories, 1905-1906, 1907-1908, 1927. Denver, Colorado: Calhoun and Holmes, 1905, 1907, 1927.

_____*1915-16*, et seq. Denver, Colorado: The Gazetteer Publishing Company, 1914-1939.

Arizona Cattlelog. Phoenix, Arizona: The Arizona Cattle Growers' Association, October 1950; April 1952; April 1953; November 1960; February, November 1965.

Ball, Larry D. *Desert Lawmen: The High Sheriffs of New Mexico and Arizona 1846-1912.* Albuquerque, New Mexico: University of New Mexico Press, 1992.

Bigando, Robert. *Globe, Arizona: The Life and Times of a Western Mining Town 1864-1917.* Globe, Arizona: Mountain Spirit Press, 1989.

Catton, Bruce. *The Civil War.* New York: American Heritage Publishing Company, 1960.

Crosswhite, Frank S. "The Annual Saguaro Harvest and Crop Cycle of the Papago, with reference to Ecology and Symbolism." *Desert Plants* 2 (Spring 1980), 3-61.

Curnow, Alice J. "Geneological [sic] Chart of My Parents," n.d.

Dedera, Don. *A Little War of Our Own.* Flagstaff, Arizona: Northland Press, 1988.

DeJong, David H. "A Scheme to Rob Them of Their Land: Water, Allotment, and the Economic Integration of the Pima Reservation, 1902-1921." *Journal of Arizona History* 44 (Summer 2003), 99-132.

Disturnell, W.C., Comp. *Arizona Business Directory and Gazetteer.* San Francisco: Bacon & Company, 1881.

Dobyns, Henry. "Who Killed the Gila?" *Journal of Arizona History* 19 (September 1978), 17-30.

Douglas [Arizona] City Directory 1930. Denver, Colorado: Gazetteer Publishing Company, 1930.

Elliott, Malinda. "Trail Into Timelessness." *American Magazine,* (November-December 1985), 55.

Goff, John. *George W.P. Hunt and His Arizona.* Pasadena, CA: Socio Technical Publications, 1973.

Granger, Byrd H., ed. *Will C. Barnes' Arizona Place Names.* Tucson, Arizona: University of Arizona Press, 1960.

Haley, James L. *Apaches: A Cultural History.* New York: Doubleday, 1981.

Hammond, George P. *Who Saw the Elephant?* California Historical Society, 1964.

Hastings, James Rodney and Raymond M. Turner. *The Changing Mile: An Ecological Study of Vegetation Change with Time in the Lower Mile of an Arid and Semiarid Region.* Tucson, Arizona: University of Arizona Press, 1965.

Haury, Emil W. *The Hohokam: Desert Farmers and Craftsmen, Excavations at Snaketown, 1964-1965.* Tucson, Arizona: University of Arizona Press, 1965.

Hoover, J.W. "The Gila River and Its Changed Character" in Indian Country of Arizona, *Geographical Review* (January 1929), 41-45.

Johnson, Allen and Dumas Malone, Ed. *Dictionary of American Biography*, Vol. 3. New York: Charles Scribner's Sons.

Levy, Joann. *They Saw the Elephant: Women in the California Gold Rush.* Hamden, Connecticut: Archon Books, 1990.

Lively, W. Irven. *The Mystic Mountains: A History of the Superstition Mountains.* W. Irven Lively, Publisher, 1955.

McNab, D. Gordon. *Those Forgotten Places: Volume 1, Arizona.* Reno, Nevada: Western Research Company, 1984.

McLoughlin, Denis. *An Encyclopedia of the Old West.* New York: Barnes & Noble, 1995.

McKenney's Pacific Coast Directory 1886-1887. San Francisco: L.M. McKenney & Company, 1886.

Miami and Globe [Arizona] City Directory 1928. Long Beach, CA: Western Directory Company, 1928.

Noble, David Grant. *Ancient Ruins of the Southwest: An Archaeological Guide.* Flagstaff, Arizona: Northland Press, 1981.

Portrait and Biographical Record of Arizona. Chicago: Chapman Publishing Company, 1901, 981.

Reisner, Marc. *Cadillac Desert: The American West and Its Disappearing Water.* New York: Penguin Books, 1986.

Report of the Governor of Arizona to the Secretary of the Interior for the year ended June 30, 1904. Washington, D.C.: GPO, 1904, 23.

Rose, Dan. *Prehistoric and Historic Gila County.* Phoenix, Arizona: Republic and Gazette Printery, 1935, 31.

San Diego, California City Directories 1907-1918, Museum of San Diego History.

Shaeffer, Margaret M. "Making an Apache Camp Dress.: U.S. Indian Service. Kinishba Ruins and Museum, Fort Apache Reservation, Arizona. (n.d.)

Summerhayes, Martha. *Vanished Arizona: Recollections of the Army Life of a New England Woman.* Salem, Massachusetts: Salem Press, 1911; reprint, Lincoln, Nebraska: University of Nebraska Press, 1979.

Swanson, James and Tom Kollenborn. *Superstition Mountain: A Ride Through Time.* Phoenix, Arizona: The Arizona Historical Foundation, 1961.

Theobald, John and Lillian. *Arizona Territorial Post Offices and Postmasters.* Phoenix, Arizona: The Arizona Historical Foundation, 1961.

Walker, Henry P. "Wagon Freighting in Arizona." *The Smoke Signal* 28. Tucson, Arizona Corral of The Westerners. (Fall 1973), 182-204.

Wilcox, David R. and Lynette O. Shenk. *The Archaeology of the Casa Grande and Its Interpretation.* Archaeology Series No. 115. Tucson, Arizona: Arizona State Museum, 1977.

Williamson, Dan R. "The Apache Kid: Red Renegade of the West." *Arizona Highways* (May 1939), 14.

Willson, Roscoe G. *Pioneer and Well Known Cattlemen of Arizona.* 2 Vol. Phoenix, Arizona: McGrew Commercial Printery, 1951, 1956.

_____. "The Apache Kid." *Arizona Days and Ways.* (April 1950).

Winsted. Manya. "Recapturing Arizona's 'Ghostly History.'" *Outdoor Arizona*, August 1972, 15.

Young, Arch Bryant, Jr. *A Social History of Early Globe, Gila County, Arizona.* A Thesis submitted to the Faculty of the Graduate School of the University of Colorado in partial fulfillment of the requirements for the Degree Master of Arts, Department of History, 1939.

Newspapers

Florence (Arizona) Enterprise, 18 July 1890.

(Globe/Miami) Arizona Silver Belt, 1881-1898; 12-15 October 1911; 30 November 1930.

_____. "Maricopa's Proposition to Drown Us Out," 31 August 1889, 3.

(Tucson, Arizona) Weekly Citizen, 29 June 1889; 16 June 1894.

(Tucson, Arizona) Daily Star, 16 March 1934.

Other Sources

Alexander, Raymond Hooper biographical file. "This Little Booklet covering the Years 1902, 1903 and 1904 is The first Portion of a Larger Work in Progress." Arizona Historical Society Library, Tucson, Arizona.

Curnow biographical file. Arizona Historical Society Library, Tucson, Arizona.

Forest Lawn Cemetery records, Los Angeles, CA.

Gila County, Arizona. Book 1 of Deeds, 535; Book 3 of Deeds, 488; Book 4 of Deeds, 20, 48; Book 5 of Deeds, 535.

Gila County, Arizona Census, 1882, #536-38.

Gila County, Arizona Jury List, 1890, #103.

Great Register of Gila County, Arizona, 1894, #154.

Great Register of Maricopa County, Arizona, 1900, #773; 1902, #1232; 1906, #997.

Lower Miami Stage Company, 1917-1926. Arizona Corporation Commission Records.

McCroskey, Mona. Notes from "Urban History in the Southwest." Graduate class at Arizona State University, Fall 1985, 48-49.

Photo Archives. Arizona Historical Society, Tucson, Arizona

Photo Archives. Arizona Collection, Hayden Library, Tempe, Arizona.

Photo Archives. Sharlot Hall Museum, Prescott, Arizona.

Sharlot Hall Collection. Archives, Sharlot Hall Museum, Prescott, Arizona.